Series Director: **Diane Larsen-Freeman**

Grammar Dimensions

Form • Meaning • Use
Workbook

Cheryl Benz
Ann Roemer

THOMSON

HEINLE

Australia • Canada • Mexico • Singapore • Spain • United Kingdom • United States

THOMSON

HEINLE

Series Director: Diane Larsen-Freeman
Grammar Dimensions 2: Form, Meaning, and Use Workbook
Cheryl Benz, Ann Roemer

Publisher: *Sherrise Roehr*
Consulting Editor: *James W. Brown*
Director of Content Development: *Anita Raducanu*
Acquisitions Editor, Academic ESL: *Tom Jefferies*
Director of Product Marketing: *Amy Mabley*
Executive Marketing Manager: *Jim McDonough*
Senior Field Marketing Manager: *Donna Lee Kennedy*
Senior Development Editor: *Michael Ryall*

Cover Image: © Rubberball Productions/Getty/RF

Editorial Assistants: *Katherine Reilly*
Senior Production Editor: *Maryellen Eschmann-Killeen*
Senior Print Buyer: *Mary Beth Hennebury*
Production Project Manager: *Chrystie Hopkins*
Production Services: *Pre-Press PMG*
Cover Designer: *Studio Montage*
Printer: *Thomson West*

Printed in the United States of America.
1 2 3 4 5 6 7 8 9 10 — 11 10 09 08 07

For more information contact Thomson Heinle, 25 Thomson Place, Boston, Massachusetts 02210 USA, or you can visit our Internet site at http://elt.thomson.com

Photo Credits: Page 1: © IndexOpen/RF
Page 14: © IndexOpen/RF
Page 26: © Comstock Images / Alamy/RF
Page 32: © PHOTOTAKE Inc. / Alamy
Page 53: (left) © Photos.com/RF (right) © John A Rizzo/Photodisc Green/Getty/RF
Page 88: © Ilene MacDonald / Alamy/RF

For permission to use material from this text or product, submit a request online at http://www.thomsonrights.com

Any additional questions about permissions can be submitted by email to thomsonrights@thomson.com

ISBN 10: 1-4240-0353-9
ISBN 13: 978-1-4240-0353-2

CONTENTS

Unit 1   Simple Present   1

Unit 2   Present Progressive and Simple Present   6

Unit 3   Talking About the Future   14

Units 1–3   Test Prep   20

Unit 4   Asking Questions   23

Unit 5   Modals of Probability and Possibility   31

Unit 6   Past Progressive and Simple Past with Time Clauses   38

Units 4–6   Test Prep   44

Unit 7   Similarities and Differences   46

Unit 8   Measure Words and Quantifiers   52

Unit 9   Degree Complements   56

Units 7–9   Test Prep   60

Unit 10   Giving Advice and Expressing Opinions   63

Unit 11   Modals of Necessity and Prohibition   72

Unit 12   Expressing Likes and Dislikes   79

Units 10–12   Test Prep   84

Unit 13   Present Perfect with *Since* and *For*   87

Unit 14   Present Perfect and Simple Past   92

Unit 15   Present Perfect Progressive   98

Units 13–15   Test Prep   102

Unit 16   Making Offers with *Would You Like*   105

Unit 17   Requests and Permission   110

Unit 18   *Used To* with *Still* and *Anymore*   115

Units 16–18   Test Prep   120

Unit 19   Past Perfect   122

Unit 20   Articles   127

Unit 21   Articles with Names of Places   134

Units 19–21   Test Prep   137

Unit 22   The Passive   140

Unit 23   Phrasal Verbs   147

Unit 24   Adjective Clauses and Participles as Adjectives   154

Unit 25   Conditionals   158

Units 22–25   Test Prep   169

SIMPLE PRESENT
Habits, Routines, and Facts

 EXERCISE 1 *(Focus 1, page 2)*

Read about the students in their writing class. Underline the verbs that tell about habits (things they do again and again, sometimes without realizing it) or routines (things they do regularly). The first one has been done for you as an example.

Writing is my favorite class because of my classmates. Even though they <u>work</u> hard to improve their writing, they like to have fun, too. Raul and Suzette study the hardest. They always listen carefully to the directions and raise their hands when they have a question. They like to help other students in the class, but they don't do the work for them. They encourage other students to write their own papers. Jean Marc is my best friend in the class. He always helps me with my writing assignments. Before I rewrite my papers, I always ask him to read them. He helps me see my mistakes.

There is only one student who doesn't participate in class—Yaniv. He always interrupts the teacher and whispers to other students. Sometimes he eats and drinks in class. Besides that, he never pays attention, and he hardly ever does his assignments.

EXERCISE 2 *(Focus 2, page 2)*

Write five sentences about habits or routines of a good student. Then write five sentences about the habits or routines of a poor student.

A Good Student

1. _____
   _____
2. _____
   _____
3. _____
   _____
4. _____
   _____
5. _____
   _____

A Poor Student

6. _____

7. _____

8. _____

9. _____

10. _____

EXERCISE 3   (Focus 2, page 2)

The following chart lists the responses of some students to a survey. Using the information on the chart, answer the questions below in complete sentences. The first one has been done for you as an example.

DO YOU . . .	YES	NO
discuss politics with native English speakers?	Raul	Yaniv
listen to the radio in English?	Valentina	Wan-Yin
watch movies or TV in English?	Mohammed	Yaniv
speak English at work or school?	Jean Marc Wan-Yin	Humberto
read English-language newspapers or magazines?	Suzette	Keiko
go to English class every day?	Maria	Tran
write letters in English?	Suzette	Raul
practice English with native speakers?	Roberto	Valentina

1. Who listens to the radio in English?

   Valentina listens to the radio in English.

2. Who writes letters in English?

   _____

3. Who doesn't read English-language newspapers or magazines?

   _____

4. Who never discusses politics with English speakers?

   _____

5. Who doesn't watch movies in English?

   _____

6. Who speaks English at work or at school?

   _____

7. Who goes to English class every day?

   _____

8. Who practices English with native speakers?

   _____

9. Who watches movies or TV in English?

   _____

10. Who never listens to the radio in English?

    _____

■ EXERCISE 4   *(Focus 2, page 2)*

With a partner, take turns asking each other the eight questions from the chart in Exercise 3. Write your partner's short answers below.

Example: You: *Do you discuss politics with native English speakers?*
         Your partner: *No, I don't.*
           You write: <u>No, she doesn't.</u>

Partner's Name _____
   1. _____
   2. _____
   3. _____
   4. _____
   5. _____
   6. _____
   7. _____
   8. _____

Now find a new partner. Tell your new partner the information you learned from your first partner.

Example: *Suzette doesn't discuss politics with native English speakers.*

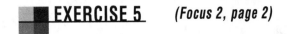

EXERCISE 5   *(Focus 2, page 2)*

Complete the puzzle below by writing in the correct form of each missing verb in the numbered sentences. The first one has been done for you as an example.

1. A spider _____has_____ eight legs.

2. A chameleon _____ its color.

3. A parrot _____ up to 50 years.

4. A fish _____ in the ocean.

5. A panda _____ bamboo sprouts.

6. A bird _____ a nest before she lays an egg.

7. A bat _____ at night.

8. A raccoon _____ a striped tail.

9. A frog _____ flies with its tongue.

10. A dolphin lives in the water, but it _____ air.

11. A bird _____ on her eggs to keep them warm.

```
                      1.  H  A  S  ③
                   2. [ ][ ]  N [ ][ ][ ] ⑦
                      3.  [ ] I [ ][ ] ⑤
                   4. [ ][ ] M [ ] ⑤
                      5.  [ ] A [ ][ ] ④
                   6. [ ][ ] L [ ][ ] ⑥
                      7.  F [ ][ ][ ][ ] ⑤
                   8. [ ] A [ ][ ] ④
                      9.  C [ ][ ][ ][ ][ ] ⑦
               10. [ ][ ][ ][ ] T [ ][ ][ ] ⑧
                      11. S [ ][ ][ ] ④
```

EXERCISE 6   (Focus 3, page 4)

Do you use several different strategies when you learn a different language, or do you depend on only one or two? Read the sentences below. For each, write the adverb of frequency that best describes your habits as you are learning English.

Example: *I usually practice saying new words in a sentence.*

1. I practice saying new words in sentences.
2. I remember new words by drawing pictures of them.
3. I try to speak like native English speakers.
4. I start conversations with native English speakers.
5. I take notes in English class.
6. I read my notes at home.
7. I try to think in English.
8. I look for similarities and differences between English and my language.
9. I ask English speakers to correct my pronunciation.
10. I try to notice my errors when I speak a language.

EXERCISE 7   (Focus 3, page 4)

Rewrite the statements from Exercise 6 as questions. Ask a partner how often he or she uses each of the different strategies. Record the answers.

Example: You ask: *How often do you practice new words in a sentence?*
         Your partner says: *I sometimes practice new words in sentences.*
              You write: She sometimes practices new words in sentences.

1. _____
2. _____
3. _____
4. _____
5. _____
6. _____
7. _____
8. _____
9. _____
10. _____

2 PRESENT PROGRESSIVE AND SIMPLE PRESENT
Actions and Styles

 EXERCISE 1   *(Focus 1, page 20)*

Read the following paragraph and underline both the present progressive and the time expression that indicates that the action is in progress at or around the time of speaking. The first one has been done for you.

Mohammed is an exchange student from Saudi Arabia who's <u>living</u> in Toronto <u>this academic year</u>. His teachers and classmates are worried about him because he looks tired and is acting differently from the way he usually acts. He's usually very outgoing, and he talks and laughs with the other students, inside the classroom and out. But these days he isn't smiling much. Normally Mohammed has lunch in the cafeteria, but today he isn't there eating. He often goes outside to smoke a cigarette, but he's not there smoking today.

    Finally someone asked Mohammed what was wrong. He explained that he is a Muslim (that is, a follower of Islam). In the lunar calendar, it's now the month of Ramadan, so he's fasting.* This month he isn't eating, drinking, or smoking during the daylight hours. The purpose of Ramadan is to teach discipline, and the fasting teaches compassion for people who are hungry and thirsty.

    Everyone at Mohammed's school is glad that he's all right and that he's just trying to be a good Muslim.

*to fast: eat or drink little or nothing

 EXERCISE 2   *(Focus 2, page 21)*

Using the present progressive verbs listed below, complete the dialogues about the following pictures. Be careful: some of them are short answers, some are negative, and others need a pronoun (*you, he, she,* etc.).

Example: *Are they taking a plane to the conference?*
                No, they're taking the train.

check	punch	type
die	quit	use
file	stand	water
fill	take	wear

1. _____
   someone _____
   those letters for me? I need them right now.
   Yes, Marcia _____.

2. Who _____ my computer?
   Dave _____.

3. Jody, _____
   those papers for Ms. Baxter?
   No, I _____.
   Jim _____.

4. That poor plant _____.
   I know. That's why I _____ it.

5. _____ in or out, sir?
   I _____ in.

6. Why _____ in line?

It's 7:00, time for the morning shift to begin.

They _____ in.

7. Where _____ Fanaye _____
out her application form?
In Human Resources.

8. What _____
for the job interview today?
I _____
a pantsuit.

9. Why _____ off his tie?
It's 5 o'clock—time to go home.

10. Why _____ his job?
Because he hates working in that company.

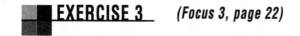

■ EXERCISE 3   *(Focus 3, page 22)*

Complete the following with the simple present (for example, *swim*) or the present progressive (for example, *be* + *swimming*), using the verbs in parentheses. The first sentence has been shown as an example.

Maria is an athlete who __is representing__ (represent) her country in the Olympic Games. She

(1) _____ (run) in the marathon, a 26.2-mile race. She usually (2) _____ (compete)

in the triathlon, which means she (3) _____ (have) to run 6.2 miles, swim 1/4 mile, and

ride a bicycle 25 miles. There's only a month to go before the Olympics, so Maria (4) _____

(train) hard to prepare. During regular training, she (5) _____ (swim) 1500 meters and

(6) _____ (run) 5 miles, but during this pre-Olympic training, she (7) _____ (swim)

less and (8) _____ (run) more. She usually (9) _____ (work) out in the weight room

an hour a day; however, this month she (10) _____ (lift) weights for two hours a day—double

her normal time. Whereas cross-country skiing is part of her winter training, now the weather is warmer

and she (11) _____ (bicycle) and roller-blading, so that different muscle groups are exercised.

Normally Maria (12) _____ (be) careful about her diet; she (13) _____ (eat) very

little fat and a lot of fruits and vegetables. Now she (14) _____ (make) extra sure that she

(15) _____ (eat) a lot of carbohydrates for energy. In addition, she (16) _____ (try)

to get plenty of sleep. She (17) _____ (be) confident that she'll be prepared, mentally and

physically, for the Olympics, and she (18) _____ (be) proud to be a part of this great event.

■ EXERCISE 4   *(Focus 3, page 22)*

Cut out a picture from a magazine or newspaper. The picture must have exactly two people in it. Also, make sure it has activities that you can describe using the present progressive. Write a description of what's happening in the photograph.

Your teacher will show several of the photographs to the entire class and read one description. Listen to each description and choose the picture that is being described.

Complete the following with the simple present (for example, *drive*) or the present progressive (for example, *be + driving*), using the verbs in parentheses.

Stewart and Annie _____*are*_____ (be) college professors. Right now it (1) _____

(be) spring break and they (2) _____ (be) on vacation. They usually (3) _____

(travel), but this year they (4) _____ (stay) home. They can't take a trip because they

(5) _____ (have) too much to take care of. They have to fix things around the house and

besides, they (6) _____ (think) it (7) _____ (be) cruel to leave their pets home alone.

They have three indoor cats. They (8) _____ (not own) a dog, but their next-door neighbor

moved away and abandoned her dog, an Alaskan Malamute named Keno. They (9) _____

(take) care of him, which (10) _____ (not be) easy because he (11) _____ (be) a

big dog and he (12) _____ (be) afraid of people. Their former neighbor, Theresa, abused the

dog. As a result, every time Stewart or Annie (13) _____ (try) to pet Keno or touch him, he

jumps away and puts his head down. He (14) _____ (think) that they're going to hit him; he

(15) _____ (not understand) kindness; he (16) _____ (know) only cruelty. Stewart

and Annie (17) _____ (try) to be patient; they _____ (treat) him with love, hoping

that someday he will trust human beings again. They (18) _____ (take) Keno for a walk every

morning and night, and they (19) _____ (play) with him in the yard every day. Out on the street,

he (20) _____ (not know) how to behave, so the couple (21) _____ (train) him.

He (22) _____ (learn), little by little, and he (23) _____ (begin) to trust them.

They say that they (24) _____ (look) for a home for him, a place where he would have lots of

room to run and people who (25) _____ (love) him. It (26) _____ (seem) to me

that Keno already (27) _____ (belong) to someone who (28) _____ (love) him.

Read the following sentences in the simple present and the present progressive. After each, check the box that indicates the meaning of the underlined verb. The first column, state/quality, includes all of the stative verbs (i.e., those expressing states or qualities—not actions).

	STATE/QUALITY/ POSSESSION	ACTION/ EXPERIENCE
1. Mark <u>looks</u> terrible today.	_____	_____
2. <u>Do</u> you <u>think</u> he has the flu?	_____	_____
3. Joe <u>is looking up</u> a word in the dictionary.	_____	_____
4. I <u>think</u> this apartment is too small.	_____	_____
5. I'<u>m thinking</u> about moving to a bigger place.	_____	_____
6. Daniel <u>has</u> a brand-new bicycle.	_____	_____
7. I'<u>m having</u> trouble with my car.	_____	_____
8. Pew! Something in the refrigerator <u>smells</u> awful.	_____	_____
9. Alonzo'<u>s</u> at the perfume counter <u>smelling</u> the colognes.	_____	_____
10. <u>Are</u> you <u>having</u> a good time on your vacation?	_____	_____
11. <u>Do</u> you <u>have</u> time to help me?	_____	_____
12. Thank you. I <u>appreciate</u> your help.	_____	_____
13. Another girlfriend?! Who'<u>s</u> he <u>seeing</u> now?	_____	_____
14. I <u>don't see</u> the logic of that argument.	_____	_____
15. Cynthia'<u>s having</u> problems with her daughter.	_____	_____

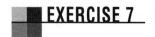

If you need help completing this crossword puzzle, ask a native speaker of English.

Across

2. Duet, trio, quartet
8. *Carmen* is an example of an _____.
10. Are you studying the piano _____ the saxophone?
12. Sheep talk
13. Shakespeare infinitive: To _____ or not to _____
14. What kind of light bulbs are you buying, Philips or General Electric? _____ (abbreviation)
15. Help! (abbreviation)
16. A repeated sound . . . sound . . . sound . . . sound . . .
19. A private, personal conversation: a _____ à tête
20. Wear: worn : : tear: _____
21. Second letter in the Greek alphabet
22. Same as 17 Down
23. Either: or : : Neither: _____
24. She's working on her PhD in Adult _____ (abbr.)
25. Sugar cane (Spanish)
29. Host of TV program (abbr.)
30. Finished (Italian)
32. The _____ in the music conservatory are excellent. I'm learning a lot from them.

Down

1. 2 Across performs this way
3. Vulgar insult (abbr.)
4. U.S. government agency that protects the environment (abbr.)
5. My fault (Latin): _____ *culpa*
6. Woman's underwear
7. Sixth note of the musical scale
9. In my class, we're writing a _____ paper on different historical periods of music.
11. That band is _____ ing a CD with Sony.
13. Soprano: top notes : : Bass: _____ notes
15. Past participle of *see*

17. Many social workers are employees of this government agency (abbr.)

18. Opposite of *off*

19. Tuberculosis (abbr.)

25. U.S. spies work for this government agency

26. Political group in South Africa

27. National Institutes of Health (abbr.)

28. Past tense of *eat*

30. Faith (Spanish)

31. Same as 10 Across

TALKING ABOUT THE FUTURE
Be Going To and Will

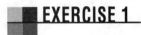 **EXERCISE 1**   *(Focus 1, page 36)*

The sentences in the paragraph below are about the future. Underline the verb form (*will* or *be going to*) and time expression that indicates the future.

Example: *Will you marry me, Nancy? I will love you for the rest of my life.*

Nancy is engaged to be married. She and her fiancé, Tim, are trying to make their wedding plans, but Nancy's mother doesn't agree with them.

Nancy's mother: Now, I have it all planned, honey. We're going to go shopping for your wedding dress this weekend. Oh, you'll look so beautiful in a long, white dress!

Nancy: Mom, I'm not going to spend hundreds of dollars on a dress that I'll never wear again.

Mother: But your father and I will pay for it!

Nancy: No, Mother. I'm going to wear a simple dress.

Tim: And I'm going to wear a suit. No rented tuxedoes for me!

Mother: Your friend Carrie has a wonderful video of her wedding. I'll call her mother this afternoon; maybe we can hire the same videographer.

Nancy: Mother! Uncle John is a photographer. I'm sure he'll take pictures, and he won't charge anything.

Mother: Now, what about the reception? We're going to have a big party with music and dancing, aren't we? We'll hire a band, and . . .

Nancy: No, Mom. Tim and I want to have something more simple. Will you and Dad have the reception at your house?

Mother: Well, it *is* traditional that the bride's parents pay for the reception . . . I'm sure it'll be OK with your father. I'll ask him tonight.

Nancy: Thanks, Mom!

EXERCISE 2 *(Focus 2, page 37)*

Work with a partner. Using the following predictions from a fortune teller, who is reading your palm, ask and answer a yes/no question about each, using *be going to* or *will*.

Example: *You will meet an interesting stranger.*
Will I meet him at school?
No, you won't. You'll meet him at a party.

1. You will take a trip before the end of next month.

   _____

   _____

2. Soon you're going to meet someone special.

   _____

   _____

3. Someone will ask you to keep a secret.

   _____

   _____

4. You're going to receive some money.

   _____

   _____

5. You will live a long and happy life.

   _____

   _____

EXERCISE 3 *(Focus 3, page 38)*

For each of the following verbs, use *will* or *be going to*, as appropriate. Use *be going to* for actions that will happen soon, and use *will* for more formal situations that will not happen soon. In some sentences, both choices are correct.

According to sociologists, some immigrant parents in North America find it difficult to let their children go away to college in another city or state/province, after they graduate from high school. It is customary to send young people away to the best possible university. North Americans feel that by going away to college, their children (1) _____ learn to be independent and self-sufficient, two qualities that are important in their culture.

These immigrant parents, however, are worried about their children's safety. They're afraid that something bad (2) _____ happen to their son or daughter and they (3) _____ (not be) able to protect them. Some parents don't think their children (4) _____ be successful on their own.

They're afraid that the young people (5) _____ fail, that they (6) _____ (not be) able to deal with everything, such as studying, doing laundry, and taking care of themselves. College officials and students say that these immigrant parents are also worried that their sons and daughters (7) _____ forget their family and (8) _____ (not want) to go back home.

Many young high-school graduates, on the other hand, want to go away to college. Giselle Siu, a senior at Houston High School, said to her parents, "Look, I (9) _____ be 18 soon and legally I (10) _____ be able to leave home, with or without your permission." Other students are more sensitive when they try to persuade their parents. Alex Iavnoski, another high-school senior who just received a letter of acceptance from the University of Iowa, told his parents, " I (11) _____ answer this letter right away and I (12) _____ say 'yes.' And with my scholarship, I (13) _____ save you money, too. Some day you (14) _____ be very proud of me." Still others don't even apply to colleges that are out of state. "My mom and dad are super strict. I know what they (15) _____ say, so I (16) _____ apply to the local community college," says Ramón Sierra.

(The above is based on "Leaving Home," Ana Veciana-Suárez, *The Miami Herald*, April 16, 1993.)

■ EXERCISE 4   *(Focus 4, page 39)*

Complete the following sentences about your future. Use *be going to* for plans and intentions, and use *will* for predictions.

Example: *As a parent, I'm never going to hit my children.*

1. As a parent, _____
   _____

2. After class today, _____
   _____

3. My horoscope today says that _____
   _____

4. After the end of this term/semester, _____
   _____

5. Next weekend, _____
   _____

6. After graduation, _____
   _____

7. Maybe on my next birthday, _____
   _____

8. Ten years from now, _____

_____

9. My fortune cookie says that _____

_____

10. On my next vacation, _____

_____

■ EXERCISE 5   *(Focus 5, page 41)*

Read the following comments from your boss. How do you respond? Use the words from the list, and respond with the correct form of *will* or *be going to*. (Remember to use *will* for quick decisions and serious promises.)

be better next year	go in July
be on time from now on	help you
call her as soon as I can	not happen again
get it right away	not tell anyone

1. "Where is that memo that I asked you to write?"

_____

2. "You were late for work three times this week."

_____

3. "When do you plan to take your vacation this year?"

_____

4. "I need someone to assist me with this special project."

_____

5. "Can you please ask Alexis if she wants to join us?"

_____

6. "Please don't tell anyone about our meeting. It's top secret."

_____

7. "Your annual evaluation was not very good, you know."

_____

8. "You were not very careful—you made a lot of mistakes on that report."

_____

Crossword puzzle

Across

1. Madame C., a gypsy, is a _____ teller who reads your palm and sees the future in her crystal ball.

6. Nickname for Albert

7. All right

9. Air conditioning (abbreviation)

11. When I first met Madame C., she was very formal and said, "How do you _____ ?"

13. Madame C., where will I be living _____ 20 years?

14. Exclamation

15. Past tense of *see*

17. Madame C. says that my children will be as American as apple _____ .

18. Madame C., when I win the lottery, will I save or _____ all the money?

19. Part of a bookcase or cabinet that holds things

20. Opposite of *always*

24. Sugar and honey taste _____ .

27. An English term for father

28. When you are critically ill, the hospital puts you in the _____ . (abbr.)

29. Madame C. says that I need a little _____ and _____ , or rest and relaxation.

30. Madame C., last night I dreamt that I was a ballerina, wearing a _____ tu.

31. Advertisement (abbr.)

33. Either: _____ : : Neither: nor

34. Madame C. predicts that I will meet one famous woman and two famous _____ .

35. An English term for mother

37. Madame C., is my life going to be full of happiness or _____ ?

Down

1. Fourth note in the musical scale

2. Opposite of *young*

3. If you are not a citizen of this country, you are a _____ citizen.

4. The abbreviation for electrocardiogram is __ __ G.

5. Madame C.'s name

8. Madame C. will tell you the past, the present, and _____. (2 words)

10. Madame C. sees someone in her crystal ball at a graduation ceremony wearing a _____ and gown.

12. 2, 4, 6, and 8 are even numbers, and 1, 3, 5, and 7 are _____ numbers.

13. Possessive of *it*

14. Petroleum

16. You and I

17. Physical education (abbr.)

21. Rabbits and elephants have big _____s.

22. Venereal disease (abbr.)

23. Madame C.'s crystal ball is not square it's _____.

24. Madame C. saw in her crystal ball that I did something bad. She said, "_____ on you!"

25. *Old McDonald had a farm, __ __, __ __ O.*

26. Prefix relating to the natural environment

30. The British are famous for their afternoon _____.

32. Two (Spanish)

34. Multiple Sclerosis (abbr.)

36. Mr.: man : : _____ : woman

Choose the word or phrase (*a, b, c,* or *d*) that best completes each sentence. Then circle the letter.

1. _____ a job yet?

   a. Does Don has

   b. Does Don have

   c. Has Don

   d. Don has

2. Yes, Don _____ in construction; he is a carpenter.

   a. doesn't work

   b. is working

   c. isn't working

   d. work

3. All the carpenters on his crew _____ new houses.

   a. build

   b. builds

   c. is building

   d. will building

4. Don says, "_____ twice and saws once."

   a. Always a good carpenter measures

   b. A good carpenter hardly measures ever

   c. A good carpenter always measures

   d. A good carpenter measures hardly ever

5. This is the reason that Don _____ costly mistakes.

   a. always make

   b. doesn't make

   c. isn't making

   d. is always make

6. As soon as I finish doing this, I _____ visit a fortuneteller.

   a. 'm going to

   b. going to

   c. will

   d. will to

7. I _____ married next month, and I want to see what the stars say about my future.

   a. am going get

   b. 'm going to get

   c. will get

   d. won't get

8. Madame Cassandra read my palm and said, "There _____ romance in your life."

   a. are going to be   c. will be

   b. not going to be   d. won't to be

9. According to the fortuneteller's crystal ball, I _____ someone new and fall in love.

   a. going to meet   c. will be meeting

   b. 'm going to meet   d. will meets

10. My fiancé found out. Now I have to promise him that _____ see Madame Cassandra anymore.

   a. I'm going to   c. I will

   b. I'm not going to   d. I won't

11. It used to be that an employee automatically retired at age 65, but nowadays people _____ off retirement, sometimes indefinitely.

   a. are putting   c. puts

   b. is putting   d. will put

12. It _____ that some people do it because they feel they need to keep busy; work has always been the center of their lives.

   a. is seeming   c. seems

   b. seem   d. will seem

13. These people don't know what to do with all the time that they now _____ during retirement.

   a. are having   c. has

   b. is having   d. have

14. Most of them _____ hobbies and they don't know how to spend all this leisure time.

   a. don't have   c. no have

   b. haven't   d. won't have

15. Other people continue working because of economic necessity—the government Social Security check _____ enough to live on.

   a. is often   c. often is

   b. is seldom   d. seldom is

Questions 16-30: Circle the *one* underlined word or phrase that must be changed or eliminated in each sentence in order for the sentence to be grammatically correct.

16. Most North American children (a) <u>begin</u> to work at home, where they (b) <u>are having</u> daily and/or weekly responsibilities, such as (c) <u>washing</u> the dishes and (d) <u>feeding</u> the dog.

17. Children (a) <u>receive</u> a weekly allowance (b) <u>often</u>, which (c) <u>is</u> a small amount of money, like a salary, in exchange (d) <u>for</u> doing these household chores or jobs.

18. The children (a) <u>are using</u> this money (b) <u>to buy</u> candy, soda, and things that (c) <u>they</u> (d) <u>need</u> for school.

19. Others (a) <u>often</u> (b) <u>save</u> (c) <u>their</u> allowance and (d) <u>making</u> bigger purchases: computer games, a pet, a musical instrument, or extra activities at summer camp.

20. The purpose of the allowance (a) <u>is</u> to teach children the value of money and to teach them responsibility—when they (b) <u>don't work</u> and do a good job, they (c) <u>aren't</u> (d) <u>receive</u> the money.

21. North Americans (a) <u>often</u> (b) <u>eat</u> out at fast-food restaurants because they (c) <u>no</u> (d) <u>have</u> time to prepare food at home.

22. These restaurants (a) <u>serve</u> almost anything: from pizza to fried chicken to good old hamburgers. Some people (b) <u>eat</u> inside, and others (c) <u>stay</u> in their car and (d) <u>buying</u> their food from the drive-through window.

23. Some Americans hardly (a) <u>never</u> (b) <u>eat</u> at home; they (c) <u>depend</u> (d) <u>on</u> these inexpensive restaurants for their meals.

24. For example, my brother (a) <u>never</u> (b) <u>prepare</u> his own food at home—he (c) <u>always</u> goes out to fast-food restaurants and (d) <u>eats</u> hamburgers and French fries.

25. (a) <u>Are</u> you (b) <u>think</u> it (c) <u>is</u> healthy (d) <u>to eat</u> that salty, processed, fried food?

26. Karen and Steve, a modern young couple, (a) <u>hardly never</u> (b) <u>do</u> anything without a plan—they (c) <u>always</u> (d) <u>talk</u> together about plans for their jobs, their home, and their family.

27. Karen (a) <u>is</u> expecting; next month she and Steve (b) <u>are going to</u> have a baby. Their doctor (c) <u>will say</u> that Karen (d) <u>is having</u> a normal pregnancy.

28. Karen and Steve (a) <u>are knowing</u> what (b) <u>they're going to</u> name the baby. If it's a girl, (c) <u>they'll</u> name her Susan, and if it's a boy, they (d) <u>will</u> name him Richard.

29. Karen (a) <u>is following</u> all the doctor's instructions. (b) <u>She's reading</u> a lot of books about pregnancy and childbirth, and she (c) <u>won't take</u> classes at the local hospital. When the time comes, (d) she<u>'ll be</u> ready.

30. It's time! Karen (a) <u>is going to</u> have her baby very soon. She (b) <u>will need</u> (c) <u>to go</u> to the hospital right now, but Steve (d) <u>can't</u> find the car keys.

ASKING QUESTIONS
Yes/No, *Wh-*, **Tag Questions,**
and Choice Questions

EXERCISE 1   *(Focus 1, page 50)*

Complete the *Yes/No* questions using the correct form of each word in parentheses, paying attention to the italicized words. Practice saying the questions with rising intonation. Then ask three of your classmates the questions. Write their names and responses on a separate sheet of paper. The first item has been completed as an example.

Questions

1. (can, swim)

    _____Can_____ you _____swim_____?

    Susan: Yes, I can.
    Anna: Yes, I can.
    Yuki: No, I can't.

2. (study)

    _____ you *usually* _____ on Saturday?

3. (live)

    _____ your family _____ in the United States *right now*?

4. (will, study)

    _____ you _____ English next year?

5. (would, help)

    _____ you _____ me?

6. (be)

    _____ English a difficult language for you?

7. (work)

    _____ you _____ *right now*?

8. (be)

    _____ I taller than you?

9. (working)

    _____ you _____ *last night*?

10. (be)

    _____ mathematics your favorite subject in elementary school?

11. (take)

_____ you _____ a vacation *last summer?*

12. (sing)

_____ you sometimes _____ in the shower?

EXERCISE 2   *(Focus 1, page 50)*

This is a *Yes/No* question game that works best with six to ten students. All students sit in a circle. One student begins by asking the student on his or her left a *Yes/No* question in the past tense. That student answers the question and then asks the student to his or her left a *Yes/No* question in the present tense. That student answers the question and then asks the student on his or her left a *Yes/No* question in the future tense. The game continues around the circle (past-tense question, present-tense question, future-tense question).

Example: Student 1: *Were you a happy child?*
Student 2: *Yes, I was. Do you usually eat meat?*
Student 3: *No, I don't. Will you get a good grade in this class?*

EXERCISE 3   *(Focus 1, page 50)*

Rewrite the questions in Exercise 1 as statement form questions. Read each question out loud. If possible, tape-record yourself and listen to make sure you are using question intonation. The first question has been written for you as an example.

1. You can swim? _____

_____

2. _____

_____

3. _____

_____

4. _____

_____

5. _____

_____

6. _____

_____

7. _____

_____

8. _____

_____

9. _____

_____

10. _____

_____

11. _____

_____

12. _____

_____

EXERCISE 4 *(Focus 2, page 52)*

Think of five things you would like to know about three of your classmates. The chart below is similar to the one in Exercise 1, but you will need to write in your own questions. Then ask your classmates the questions and write their answers on the chart.

Examples: *What is your favorite holiday in your home country?*
How many brothers and sisters do you have?

QUESTION	NAME	NAME	NAME
1.			
2.			
3.			
4.			
5.			

Verdieu Lucas is interviewing for a job as the director of the computer lab. Based on Verdieu's answers, write the questions the interviewer asks Verdieu. The first one has been done for you as an example.

Interviewer: <u>Which job are you applying for?</u>

Verdieu: I'm applying for the lab director's position.

Interviewer: _____

_____

Verdieu: I think my strong points are that I know a lot about computers and that I get along well with other people. Here's a copy of my résumé.

Interviewer: _____

_____

Verdieu: I'm looking for a full-time position. However, I'm willing to accept a part-time position to begin with.

Interviewer: _____

Verdieu: I left my last job one month ago.

Interviewer: _____

Verdieu: I left that job because my family moved here from Boston.

Interviewer: _____

Verdieu: You can see from my résumé that I worked as assistant director in the math computer lab at Bunker Hill Community College.

Interviewer: _____

Verdieu: I will be available to work just about anytime; however, I prefer to work during the day.

Interviewer: _____

Verdieu: I have my own car, so getting to work isn't a problem.

Interviewer: _____

Verdieu: I can start working right away.

Interviewer: _____

Verdieu: I expect about 15 dollars per hour.

■ EXERCISE 6   *(Focus 2, page 52)*

Choose one of the following jobs and role-play a job interview with a partner.

restaurant server	mail carrier
accountant	carpenter
medical receptionist	gas station attendant
taxi driver	singer in a nightclub
hotel desk clerk	driver for a florist
teacher's aide	salesclerk in a department store

Example: *Why do you want to work at this restaurant?*
Where have you worked before?
When can you start working?

■ EXERCISE 7   *(Focus 3, page 54)*

Write two questions for each sentence, using the underlined words for cues. The first one has been done for you as an example.

Right now, Glenn lives with his parents.

1. Who lives with his parents?
2. Whom does Glenn live with?

He will start at the university in two months.

3. _____

4. _____

He went with his uncle to look for an apartment.

5. _____

6. _____

They found a nice apartment near the university, but it was a little expensive.

7. _____

8. _____

Glenn needs a roommate.

9. _____

10. _____

Glenn called several friends.

11. _____

12. _____

Sean also needed a roommate.

13. _____

14. _____

Glenn will share his apartment with Sean.

15. _____

16. _____

EXERCISE 8   (Focus 3, page 54)

Information Gap Activity: You know some things about Laura's brothers and sister, but you get her family members mixed up. Look at the list below while your partner looks at page 29. Ask your partner "who" questions about Laura's brothers and sister using prompts 1–8. Your partner will respond with information from the next page. Then change roles. Your partner will ask you questions about prompts 9–16. You will respond with information from the next page.

Example: A: *Who is the tallest?*
               B: *Ken is the tallest.*

1. tallest
2. oldest
3. play basketball in high school (past)
4. visit Korea last year
5. start college next year

6. youngest
7. like Chinese food
8. have children
9. like sports
10. middle child
11. married

12. single
13. pilot
14. artistic
15. sings
16. shortest

KEN

JOY

BILL

Ken	Joy	Bill
26 years old/6 feet 3 inches tall	24 years old/5 feet 8 inches tall	18 years old/6 feet tall
married with two children	single	single
played basketball in high school	loves to travel	collects insects
likes all kinds of sports	went to Korea last year	paints, draws, and sings
pilot	likes Chinese food	entering college next year

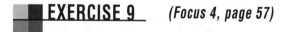 **EXERCISE 9** *(Focus 4, page 57)*

Work with a partner. Practice asking and answering the questions in Exercise 8. Ask the questions in Exercise 8 as though you were not sure what you heard.

Complete the following dialogues by adding the tag questions and completing the responses. The first one has been done for you.

DIALOGUE 1

Catherine: You're taking a math class now, ___aren't you___?

Jim: Yes, _____.

Catherine: Diana is in your class, _____?

Jim: Yes, _____.

Catherine: You both have to study a lot for that calculus class, _____?

Jim: Yes, _____.

Catherine: You'll finish that class soon, _____?

Jim: Yes, _____.

Catherine: Only three more weeks! Great. You're going to take a vacation after that, _____?

Jim: Yes, _____. I'm going to visit my family.

Catherine: Oh, I know you'll enjoy that.

DIALOGUE 2

Guillermo: You don't have any aspirin, _____? I have a giant headache.

Chris: No, sorry _____. You aren't getting sick, _____? You don't look so good.

Guillermo: No, I'm all right.

Chris: You didn't eat very much today, _____?

Guillermo: No, that's not the problem. I was working on the computer all day, and my eyes are tired.

Chris: Oh, that's the problem. You're right. You need some aspirin.

Guillermo: The pharmacy down the street is open until 10:00, _____?

Chris: Yes, I think _____. But I don't think you should go. Let me go buy something for your headache.

Guillermo: Okay. Let me get you some money. I think five dollars should be enough, _____?

Chris: Sure. That's more than enough.

■ **EXERCISE 11** *(Focus 7, page 63)*

Read the dialogues in Exercise 10 with a partner. Read the first dialogue as though you are sure what your partner's answer will be. Read the second dialogue as though you are unsure. If possible, tape-record yourself and listen to see whether your intonation is rising or falling.

MODALS OF PROBABILITY AND POSSIBILITY

Could, May, Might, Must, Couldn't, and Can't

■ **EXERCISE 1**   *(Focus 1, page 72)*

You have found a purse containing the items listed below. Circle the best answer in each space to complete the statements about the owner of the purse. Be prepared to explain your answers.

1. a driver's license with a female photo and name
   The owner of the purse ——————— a woman.
   a. could be   b. is   c. may be

2. a comb with gray hairs
   She ——————— an older woman.
   a. could be   b. might be   c. must be

3. a government employee ID card
   She ——————— for the government.
   a. could work   b. may work   c. must work

4. an iPod with music by Bach, Beethoven, and Haydn
   She ——————— like classical music.
   a. can't   b. could   c. must

5. a flash drive, CD, and PalmPilot
   She ——————— be computer literate.
   a. can't   b. might   c. must

6. pictures of children
   The children ——————— her grandchildren, or they ——————— her nieces and nephews.
   a. are   b. could be   c. might be

7. a glasses case
   She ——————— wear glasses, but the case ——————— be for sunglasses.
   a. could   b. may   c. must

8. a bank statement showing a balance of $0.00.
   She ——————— have any money in the bank account, but she ——————— have another account.
   a. could   b. doesn't   c. must

9. an Irish passport full of stamps

She _____ be American. She _____ travel a lot.

    a. might   b. must   c. must not

10. a small handgun (pistol)

She _____ work for the police. She _____ be a spy.

    a. could   b. might   c. must

EXERCISE 2   *(Focus 2, page 74)*

Unscramble the following statements of probability/possibility about some classmates.

Example: *Lee hasn't smiled all day.*

        a / bad / be / he / in / mood / must   *He must be in a bad mood.*

1. Every time I see Gigi, she's eating a candy bar.

    chocolate / like / must / she   _____

2. Every day Julia wears scrubs and clogs to class.

    a / be / might / nurse / she   _____

3. Juan always carries a helmet.

    a / he / motorcycle / must / ride   _____

4. Oleg and Natalya have the same last name and come to class together.

    be / must / related / they   _____

5. Oleg is 19 years old and Natalya is 27.

    be / couldn't / mother / Natalya / Oleg's   _____

6. Is Lin's study group going to meet this week?
I don't know.

    because / is / Lin / not / may / sick / they   _____

7. Jacques gets up in the middle of class and leaves the room.

    he / know / may / not / rude / that / that's   _____

8. Nancy wears a diamond ring, and she's always talking about a man named Tim.

    be / married / must / she   _____

9. Claudia's family has a car, but she walks to school or takes the bus.

    drive / how / know / might / not / she / to   _____

10. Who is that new student? I never saw her before.

    be / class / could / in / she / the / wrong   _____

Now, using *could*, *may*, *might*, or *must*, make three statements of probability/possibility about your own classmates. Be ready to support the statement with specific observations.

1. _____
2. _____
3. _____

EXERCISE 3   *(Focus 3, page 77)*

After reading the following dialogue, rewrite the parts in bold print, using *could*, *may*, *might*, or *must*, and the verb. Be careful—some are in the present and others are in the past. The first one has been done for you.

Gladys and her husband, Norman, are talking about their neighbors. Gladys is convinced that they are terrible people, but Norman isn't so sure. He thinks that Gladys is being a nosy neighbor and jumping to conclusions.

Gladys: Have you seen the car that the Riccios are driving? It's a Mercedes Benz! He's a handyman and she's a secretary. **It's not possible for them to make enough money** to afford that car. **They are probably drug dealers.**
          They couldn't make enough money . . . _____
          _____

Norman: Oh, Gladys. Mind your own business. **Maybe they inherited the money,** or **it's possible that they won the car** in a contest. We don't know!
          _____
          _____

Gladys: And did you see their recycling container last week? **It looked like there was a dozen wine bottles. I think they are alcoholics.**
          _____
          _____

Norman: Oh, Gladys. Mind your own business. **It's possible that the Riccios had a party,** or **maybe they invited friends over for dinner.**
          _____
          _____

Gladys: Oh, yeah? Well, two weeks ago I saw their car parked in front of St. Jude's church. **Kathy probably went to** one of those AA (Alcoholics Anonymous) meetings that they hold there.
          _____

Norman: Gladys, you don't know that for sure. **Maybe she was** at a store near the church. Mind your own business.
          _____

Gladys: Norman . . . Have you seen their little boy lately? He has cuts and bruises all over his body. **I think Tim got drunk** and hit him. That's child abuse.

_____

Norman: Gladys, it's possible the boy fell off his bike. You know how kids are. Mind your own business.

_____

Gladys: Norman . . .

Norman: Gladys, **I think you're crazy.** You haven't even met those people!

_____

Gladys: Norman, **maybe you're right.**

_____

 EXERCISE 4 _(Focus 4, page 79)_

Using the following information and pictures, complete the sentences with _could, may, might,_ **or** _must_ **in the progressive. Be careful—some of them are negative.**

Jonathan, a college student, arrives at his family's home to pay them a surprise visit. He's worried because no one is there. As he looks around the house, he's guessing what his family is doing and what they were doing right before he arrived.

Present progressive: to make a guess or draw a conclusion about something in progress at the time of speaking.

1. Dad sometimes takes an afternoon nap.

   He _____ a nap.

2. But Dad's shoes aren't by the front door. When he comes home, he always takes off his shoes and leaves them by the front door.

   He _____ a nap.

3. The grocery list is not on the refrigerator, where my sister always puts it.

My sister _____ grocery shopping.

4. But the family car and my sister's bicycle are in the garage.

My sister _____ grocery shopping.

5. Sparky, the family pet, isn't here. His leash is gone. My mom, dad, sister, and brother aren't here. The car and bikes are in the garage. The family walks Sparky every day.

Everybody _____

Past Progressive: to make a guess or draw a conclusion about something that was in progress before the time of speaking.

6. My mom's coffee cup is half empty, and it's still warm.

She _____

7. The chess set is on the table—my sister and brother often play together.

They _____

8. Dad's glasses and a book are next to his favorite chair.

He _____

9. My sister's roller blades are by the door.

She _____

10. There are a lot of cigarette butts in the ashtray, and the house smells awful.

Someone _____

Choose the best answer and write it in the space.

1. **A:** What are you going to do this weekend?
   B: My brother has tickets to the baseball game, so I _____ with him. My favorite team is playing.

   a. could go   b. 'll probably go   c. must go

2. **A:** What are you going to do on your vacation?
   B: I'm not sure. We _____ take a trip to Kenya and go on a safari.

   a. 'll probably   b. may   c. must

3. **A:** Do you have plans for tonight?
   B: Not really. I _____ just stay home and watch TV, as usual.

   a. can't   b. 'll probably   c. must

4. **A:** I wonder why Mike is wearing that bandage around his wrist.
   B: I don't know. He _____ it.

   a. might hurt   b. must have hurt   c. must hurt

5. **A:** Where are my keys?
   B: You _____ them in the kitchen.

   a. may leave   b. might have left   c. must leave

6. **A:** I haven't been feeling well lately, especially in the morning.
   B: Really? You _____ pregnant. Maybe you've got morning sickness.

   a. could be   b. 'll probably be   c. must be

7. **A:** Have you seen Lourdes?
   B: Yes, and judging from the size of her stomach, she _____ at least eight months' pregnant.

   a. could have been   b. 'll probably be   c. must be

8. **A:** Are you going to visit your family this year?
   B: I don't know. It depends on the airfares. I _____.

   a. could be   b. may be   c. might

9. **A:** What grade do you think you'll get in this class?
   B: So far I have a pretty good average, and I've been studying a lot this semester.
   I _____ get a B.

   a. can't   b. 'll probably   c. must

10. **A:** Her hair always looks so stiff and thick.
    B: I know. It looks very unnatural.
    A: She _____ wear a wig.

    a. can   b. 'll probably   c. must

PAST PROGRESSIVE AND SIMPLE PAST WITH TIME CLAUSES

When, While, and *As Soon As*

EXERCISE 1   *(Focus 1, page 90)*

THE GENTLEMAN PURSE THIEF

Imagine that you are the following victims of the Gentleman Purse Thief. Use the pictures to explain to the police what happened when the thief stole your purse. Using the past progressive (*was/were talking*) or simple past (*talked*), write your answers to the questions below. The first one is done for you.

CASE 1

VERONICA RIO

1. Miss Rio, what were you doing at the time of the robbery?
   <u>I was having a drink at the Yacht Club.</u>

2. Please describe the man who stole your purse.
   _____

3. What did you do immediately after the thief stole your purse?
   _____

CASE 2

EVA GALOR

4. Mrs. Galor, where were you and what were you doing at the time of the crime?

_____

5. Could you give us a description of the thief?

_____

6. Did the thief have a mustache?

_____

7. What did you do immediately after the thief stole your purse?

_____

CASE 3

8. Mrs. Rox, what were you ladies doing when the thief stole your purse?

_____

9. What did the thief look like?

_____

10. What was he wearing?

_____

11. Did he speak with an accent?

_____

12. What did you all do after he took your purse?

_____

■■**EXERCISE 2**   *(Focus 2, page 91)*

Imagine that you were at the bank when a robbery occurred. Test your observation skills by studying the following picture for two minutes. Then, using the past progressive, write as many sentences as you can about what was happening at the time of the robbery. Try to come up with at least ten sentences.

1. _____

_____

2. _____

_____

3. _____

_____

4. _____

_____

5. _____

_____

6. _____

_____

7. _____

_____

8. _____

_____

9. _____

_____

10. _____

_____

EXERCISE 3   *(Focus 2, page 91)*

Using the picture of the bank from Exercise 2, complete the following conversation between a detective and one of the bank tellers. Use the past progressive or the simple past, depending on the question.

1. **Detective:** Where was the manager at the time of the robbery? What was the manager doing?

   Teller: _____

   _____

2. **Detective:** Was the security guard there? What was he doing?

   Teller: _____

   _____

3. **Detective:** Were there any other employees in the bank? What were they doing?

   Teller: _____

   _____

4. **Detective:** Were any customers standing in line? If so, how many?

   Teller: _____

   _____

5. **Detective:** Please describe the person who was first in line.

   Teller: _____

   _____

6. **Detective:** Please describe the person who was last in line.

   Teller: _____

   _____

7. **Detective:** Was anyone acting suspiciously?

   (*acting suspiciously:* appearing to be doing something wrong)

   Teller: _____

   _____

8. **Detective:** What time was it?

   Teller: _____

   _____

9. **Detective:** You said that there was a man outside the door. What was he wearing?

   Teller: _____

   _____

10. **Detective:** What were *you* doing at the time of the robbery?

    Teller: _____

    _____

■ EXERCISE 4   *(Focus 3, page 92)*

Using the pictures from Exercise 1, The Gentleman Purse Thief, indicate if the following statements are true (T) or false (F). If the statement is false, reword it to make it true, using *when*, *while*, or *as soon as*.

1. Veronica Rio kissed the thief when he stole her purse.   T   F

2. Ms. Rio had a drink as soon as the thief took her purse.   T   F

3. While Veronica was having a drink, the Gentleman Purse Thief began to talk to her.   T   F

4. While Eva Galor was shouting, the thief took her purse.   T   F

5. The thief was wearing sunglasses and a hat when the second robbery took place.   T   F
   (*took place:* happened)

6. As soon as the thief took her purse, Eva said "Thank you."   T   F

7. Mrs. Rox and her friends were playing bridge when the third crime took place.   T   F
   (*bridge:* a card game)

8. As soon as the Gentleman Purse Thief took their purses, the ladies played bridge.   T   F

9. The thief was probably wearing a disguise when he committed these crimes.   T   F
   (*disguise:* something to change his appearance)

10. While the Gentleman Purse Thief was committing his crimes, he was rude to his victims.   T   F

Rewrite the sentences from Exercise 4, changing the order of the clauses and the punctuation. The first one is done for you.

1. When the thief stole her purse, Veronica Rio ran after him. _____
   _____
   _____

2. _____
   _____
   _____

3. _____
   _____
   _____

4. _____
   _____
   _____

5. _____
   _____
   _____

6. _____
   _____
   _____

7. _____
   _____
   _____

8. _____
   _____
   _____

9. _____
   _____
   _____

10. _____
   _____
   _____

TEST PREP

Choose the word or phrase (*a, b, c,* or *d*) that best completes each sentence. Then circle the letter.

1. Emily needed some money yesterday to buy gas for her car, so she _____ to the bank.
    a. didn't go
    b. could have gone
    c. was going
    d. went

2. _____ Emily was getting cash at an ATM, someone came up behind her and robbed her.
    a. After
    b. As soon as
    c. Before
    d. While

3. The thief _____ a T-shirt and blue jeans and had big tattoos all over his arms.
    a. was wearing
    b. weared
    c. may have worn
    d. might worn

4. He was holding something in his hand. Emily thought that it _____ a gun.
    a. could be
    b. could been
    c. may have been
    d. was being

5. _____ she realized what happened, Emily ran to her car, called the police on her cell phone, and reported the crime.
    a. As soon as
    b. Before
    c. During
    d. While

6. The first question that the police asked her was _____.
    a. "You are OK, Ma'am, are you?"
    b. "Would you be OK, Ma'am?"
    c. "Are you OK, Ma'am?"
    d. "You could be OK, Ma'am, couldn't you?"

7. The second question that the police asked was _____.
    a. "What did happen?"
    b. "What's happening?"
    c. "What must have happened?"
    d. "What happened?"

8. Then they asked her _____.
    a. "How much money could he take?"
    b. "How much money did he take?"
    c. "How much money was he taking?"
    d. "How much money he took?"

9. Emily was lucky because her keys were still in her pocket. With her keys, the thief _____ her car.

    a. could have stolen   c. was stealing

    b. must have stolen   d. stole

10. But the thief stole her money and her credit cards. Without money, Emily _____ buy gas, and she had to walk home.

    a. could   c. might

    b. couldn't   d. might not

11. Later, the police told Emily that she hadn't been very careful. The thief was standing near the bank and she _____ noticed him.

    a. could   c. must

    b. could have   d. must have

12. They also told her that she was very lucky. She _____ hurt very seriously.

    a. could been   c. might have been

    b. may be   d. must be

13. Two days later, someone _____ Emily's purse, with all of her identification and credit cards, in a trash can.

    a. may have found   c. was finding

    b. found   d. was found

14. The police called Emily and told her the good news. "All in all, you are a very lucky lady, Ms. O'Hara, _____?

    a. do you   c. are you

    b. don't you   d. aren't you

EDITING PRACTICE

Questions 15-19: Circle the *one* underlined word or phrase that must be changed for the sentence to be grammatically correct.

15. A 28-year-old woman (a) <u>may become</u> the next princess. The prince (b) <u>was made</u> his decision (c) <u>after</u> he (d) <u>consulted</u> his list of more than 100 candidates.

16. At first, the prince's first choice (a) <u>didn't</u> want to be on the "princess list." People (b) <u>said</u> that she (c) <u>must</u> (d) <u>had</u> a boyfriend.

17. But the prince (a) <u>started</u> calling her on the telephone every day. He (b) <u>must have been</u> very convincing. The future princess <u>is</u> a very independent and well-educated woman. Princesses in the past (b) <u>were</u> very traditional women. She (c) <u>may</u> (d) <u>be changed</u> the very conservative role of princess.

18. (a) <u>While</u> she (b) <u>was living</u> in Australia, she (c) <u>was worked</u> as a diplomat. She speaks five languages and (d) <u>studied</u> in four countries.

19. (a) <u>Why</u> do you think about the prince's choice? (b) <u>Do</u> you think he (c) <u>made</u> the right decision? (d) <u>Do</u> you think the princess will be happy?

SIMILARITIES AND DIFFERENCES
Comparatives, Superlatives,
As . . . As, Not As . . . As

 EXERCISE 1 *(Focus 1, page 106)*

Psychologists doing research on the brain find that some people use the right side of their brain more than the left side. Other people depend more on the left side of the brain when they have to solve a problem or learn something. A third group of people have no clear preference; they use both sides of the brain equally. The chart below shows some of the different characteristics of "right-brain" and "left-brain" people. Using the information from the chart, complete the sentences on the next page with the appropriate form of the comparative or superlative. The first one is an example.

Left-Brain	Right-Brain
Logical, rational	Artistic, emotional
Verbal—good speaking skills	Nonverbal
Worry about details	Look at the "whole picture"
Conservative	Liberal
Want to be in control	Take risks*
Neat, organized	Look unorganized, but know where things are
Always on time or early	Rarely on time
Competitive	Cooperative
Good at algebra	Good at geometry
Make lists of day's activities	Picture (that is, "see in their mind") places, people, things they have to do
After meeting someone for the first time, they remember the person's name	After meeting someone for the first time, they remember the person's face
When shopping, they buy after reading labels, comparing prices	When shopping, they buy on impulse
When explaining a plan, they do it orally	When explaining a plan, they prefer to use paper and pencil
Prefer to work alone	Outgoing and work well with others
Enjoy sewing and/or chess	Enjoy skiing and/or swimming
Enjoy doing crossword puzzles	Enjoy fishing and/or running
Like to plan trips	Like surprises
Like to fix things around the house	Like to rearrange furniture at home

* *a risk*: a chance, danger of losing something important

LEFT-BRAIN PEOPLE

1. They are _____*less*_____ emotional _____*than*_____ right-brain people.

2. They speak _____ skillfully _____ right-brain people.

3. They shop _____ carefully _____ people in the right-brain category.

4. The _____ competitive individuals of all are left-brain dominant.

5. They are _____, or more organized, _____ right-brain people.

6. They like to fix things _____ right-brain people do.

RIGHT-BRAIN PEOPLE

7. They are _____ artistic _____ left-brain people.

8. They probably have _____ friends _____ people in the other two categories.

9. They are _____ punctual _____ left-brain people.

10. They are _____ cooperative _____ people in the first group.

11. They like surprises _____ left-brain people do.

12. The _____ outgoing people of all the groups are in this category.

Check (✓) your personal preferences in the chart below. Count the total number of check marks you have in each category to decide if you are left- or right-brain dominant. Compare your answers with your classmates'. Then, using the comparative and superlative forms, write sentences comparing yourself with the other members of the group.

Left	Right	No Preference
____ I'm logical and rational.	____ I'm artistic and emotional.	____
____ I'm verbal; I speak well.	____ I'm nonverbal.	____
____ I worry about details.	____ I look at the "whole picture."	____
____ I'm conservative.	____ I'm liberal.	____
____ I want to be in control.	____ I take risks.	____
____ I'm neat and organized.	____ I seem unorganized, but I know where things are.	____
____ I'm on time or early.	____ I'm rarely on time.	____
____ I'm competitive.	____ I'm cooperative.	____
____ I'm good at algebra.	____ I'm good at geometry.	____
____ I make lists of my day's activities.	____ I picture (that is, "see in my mind") my day's activities.	____
____ After I meet someone for the first time, I remember the person's name.	____ After I meet someone for the first time, I remember the person's face.	____
____ When I'm shopping, I buy after reading the labels and comparing prices.	____ When I'm shopping, I buy on impulse.	____
____ To explain a plan, I prefer to speak.	____ To explain a plan, I prefer to use a pencil and paper.	____
____ I prefer to work alone.	____ I'm outgoing and work well with others.	____
____ I enjoy sewing and/or chess.	____ I enjoy skiing and/or swimming.	____
____ I like doing crossword puzzles.	____ I like fishing and/or running.	____
____ I like to plan trips.	____ I like surprises.	____
____ I like to fix things around the house.	____ I like to rearrange the furniture at home.	____
____ Total	____ Total	____ Total

Examples: *Susan is more artistic than I.*
I take more risks than Susan and Mark.
Mark is the most competitive person in the group.

1. _____

_____

2. _____

_____

3. _____

_____

4. _____
   _____

5. _____
   _____

6. _____
   _____

7. _____
   _____

8. _____
   _____

9. _____
   _____

10. _____
    _____

■ EXERCISE 3   *(Focus 1, page 106)*

Pilar is tired of taking the bus to work and school. She is thinking about buying a car, a scooter, or a bicycle. Using the information below, complete her sentences. Write the appropriate comparative or superlative form of the word in parentheses.

Example: *A bicycle is much cheaper than a car.*

Insurance: $550/year
Gas Mileage: 15 mpg

Insurance: $275/year
Gas Mileage: 50 mpg

1. Of the three types of transportation, a car costs _____ (more), and a bicycle costs _____ (less).

2. The insurance for a car is _____ (high) than the insurance for a scooter.

3. The gas mileage for a car is _____ (bad) that for a scooter. A bike is _____ (good) because it doesn't need any gas at all.

4. All in all, a car is _____ (expensive), and a bicycle is _____ (expensive).

5. A bicycle is much _____ (light) a scooter; I could carry it up the stairs and keep it in my apartment.

6. A car is _____ (heavy) a bike or a scooter, but that's why it's _____ (safe), too.

7. Yes, but with a car I have to worry about parking. Both a bike and a scooter are _____ (easy) to park.

8. A scooter is _____ (fun) a car, but it's also _____ (dangerous).

9. The _____ (healthy) choice is a bicycle. It's good exercise for me, and it's good for the environment. Of the three choices, it's _____ (expensive) as well.

10. If I buy a car, I can save much _____ (more) money _____ if I buy a bicycle.

■ EXERCISE 4 *(Focus 2, page 108)*

Circle T if the statement is true and F if the statement is false. Use the information from Exercise 3.

1. The gas mileage for a car is almost as low as the gas mileage for a scooter.	T	F
2. A car is just about as economical as a bicycle.	T	F
3. A bike isn't as heavy as a scooter.	T	F
4. A bicycle doesn't cost nearly as much as a car.	T	F
5. Riding a bike is practically as cheap as taking the bus.	T	F
6. When traffic is heavy, a bicycle would be just about as fast as a car.	T	F
7. It is not as easy to find parking for a bicycle as it is for a car.	T	F
8. A scooter has nowhere near as much cargo space as a car.	T	F
9. When it rains, a scooter is almost as bad as a bike, if not worse.	T	F
10. I can give nearly as many people a ride in a car as on a scooter.	T	F

■ EXERCISE 5 *(Focus 3, page 110)*

Using the information from the chart in Exercise 1, complete the following sentences about Lois, a left-brain person, and Roy, a right-brain person. Use *less than*, *more than*, and *as . . . as*, and complete the sentence, if necessary.

Example: *Lois's house is probably cleaner than Roy's.*

1. Roy seems to be _____ organized _____ Lois.

2. Roy's closets probably aren't _____ neat _____ Lois's _____.

3. Lois doesn't take _____ risks as Roy _____.

4. Roy isn't _____ good at remembering names _____ Lois _____.

5. Of all her friends, Lois is _____ mechanical and _____ artistic.

6. Roy isn't _____ conservative _____ most of his friends.

7. Lois doesn't have _____ friends _____ Roy _____.

8. Lois probably doesn't like fishing _____ much _____ Roy _____.

9. Roy doesn't talk _____ much _____ Lois _____.

10. Roy likes decorating his house _____ Lois _____.

EXERCISE 6   *(Focus 4, page 113)*

You are a teacher and you have to talk to the parents of one of your students. Which of the following is the polite and less direct way to compare their son, Johnny, with his classmates? Put a check mark (✓) next to the more polite form.

1. _____ Mr. and Mrs. Callahan, Johnny is not doing as well as the other students.

   _____ Mr. and Mrs. Callahan, Johnny is doing much worse than the other students.

2. _____ Johnny doesn't seem to study as much as the other boys and girls.

   _____ Johnny seems to study much less than the other boys and girls.

3. _____ Johnny's classmates concentrate more than he does in class.

   _____ Johnny doesn't concentrate as much as his classmates.

4. _____ The other students' spelling isn't as bad as Johnny's.

   _____ Johnny's spelling isn't as good as the other students'.

5. _____ When learning new lessons, the other boys and girls aren't as slow as Johnny.

   _____ When learning new lessons, Johnny isn't as fast as the other boys and girls.

6. _____ Johnny is less cooperative than his classmates.

   _____ Johnny isn't quite as cooperative as his classmates.

7. _____ The other boys and girls don't read as slowly as Johnny.

   _____ Johnny doesn't read as fast as the other boys and girls.

8. _____ The other students aren't as impolite as Johnny.

   _____ Johnny isn't as polite as the other students.

9. _____ In music class, the other boys and girls sing better than Johnny.

   _____ In music class, Johnny doesn't sing as well as the other boys and girls.

10. _____ All in all, Johnny is the worst student in the class.

    _____ All in all, Johnny isn't doing quite as well as his classmates.

MEASURE WORDS AND QUANTIFIERS

■ EXERCISE 1   *(Focus 1, page 122)*

Mrs. Griffin sent her husband shopping, but he ripped the shopping list. Can you help Mr. Griffin by completing the list? The first one has been done for you.

Grocery List

1. <u>a bunch</u>  _____ of bananas

2. _____ of bread

3. _____ eggs

4. _____ of lettuce

5. _____ of mayonnaise

6. _____ of dog food

7. _____ of cereal

8. _____ of radishes

9. _____ of white wine

10. _____ of ice cream

I went next door to borrow . . .

This is a game to test your memory. All players should sit in a circle. The first player begins by saying, "I went next door to borrow a can of anchovies" (or a bag of apples—any food that begins with the letter "A"). The second player repeats what the first player says and then adds another item, which begins with the letter "B." "I went next door to borrow a can of anchovies and a loaf of bread." The third player must repeat what the first two players have said and add another item, which begins with "C." "I went next door to borrow a can of anchovies, a loaf of bread, and a piece of cake," and so on until the whole alphabet has been completed.

EXERCISE 3 *(Focus 2, page 125)*

Look at the grocery list in Exercise 1. Some of the items are count nouns (bananas) and some are noncount (bread). Write "C" beside each count noun and "NC" beside each noncount noun.

EXERCISE 4 *(Focus 2, page 125)*

Using the food and measure words as cues, write the correct measure phrases to complete the following recipes. The first one has been done for you as an example.

AVOCADO ICE CREAM

2 _____cups of milk_____ *(milk, cup)*

1/2 _____ *(granulated sugar, cup)*

1/4 _____ *(salt, teaspoon)*

2 _____ *(egg)*

1 _____ *(heavy cream, cup)*

2 _____ *(lemon extract, teaspoon)*

1 _____ *(mashed avocado, cup)*

- *Combine milk, sugar, and salt; scald. Pour over eggs, stirring constantly. Add cream and lemon extract and cool.*

- *Add avocado and mix thoroughly. Freeze in ice-cream freezer. Makes about 1 quart.*

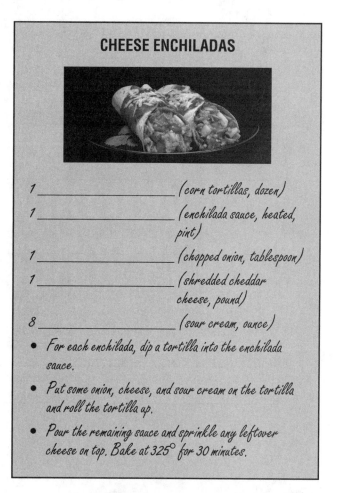

CHEESE ENCHILADAS

1 _____ *(corn tortillas, dozen)*

1 _____ *(enchilada sauce, heated, pint)*

1 _____ *(chopped onion, tablespoon)*

1 _____ *(shredded cheddar cheese, pound)*

8 _____ *(sour cream, ounce)*

- *For each enchilada, dip a tortilla into the enchilada sauce.*

- *Put some onion, cheese, and sour cream on the tortilla and roll the tortilla up.*

- *Pour the remaining sauce and sprinkle any leftover cheese on top. Bake at 325° for 30 minutes.*

Look at the series of pictures below. Write a sentence describing each picture using a common quantifier. The first one has been done for you as an example. (Remember, *juice*, a noncount noun; *children*, a count noun.)

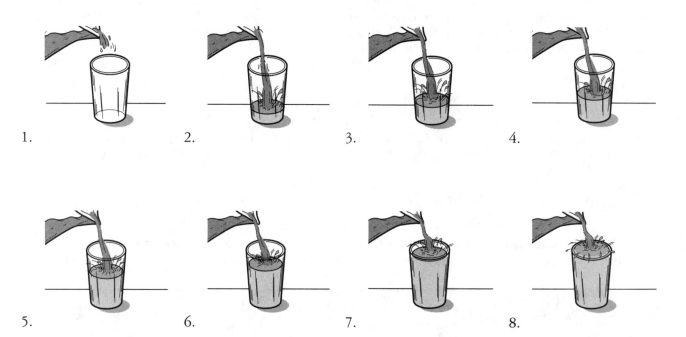

1.   2.   3.   4.

5.   6.   7.   8.

1. <u>There is no juice in the glass.</u>

2. _____

3. _____

4. _____

5. _____

6. _____

7. _____

8. _____

1.

2.

3.

4.

5.

6.

1. <u>All of the children</u> _____ are in the swimming pool.

2. _____ are in the swimming pool.

3. _____ are diving into the pool.

4. There are _____ in the pool.

5. _____ are lying next to the pool.

6. _____ are out of the pool.

7.

8.

9.

7. There are _____ in the pool.

8. There are _____ in the pool.

9. There are _____ in the pool.

UNIT 9

DEGREE COMPLEMENTS
Too, Enough, and Very

EXERCISE 1   *(Focus 1, page 138)*

The Ganter family members have just moved to Nashville. They have three young children, and they are looking for a house, but they don't think that they have enough money to buy a new house. The following is a list of characteristics they gave their realtor, to provide the features they are looking for in a house:

about $200,000   two bathrooms
older house   large yard
four bedrooms   good school district

Their realtor gave them descriptions of the following houses. What do you think the Ganters said about each house? Write *enough*, *not enough*, or *too*, as appropriate, in each blank.

Example: *There are not enough bathrooms.*

Modern, beautiful home with all the conveniences: deluxe dishwasher, washer, dryer, side-by-side refrigerator and freezer. Three bedrooms, one bath. Small lot. $245,000.

1. The house is _____ modern.

2. There are _____ bedrooms.

3. The yard is _____ large _____.

4. The house is not _____ expensive.

Built in 1926, this fixer-upper is loaded with space! Large lot. Four large bedrooms, two bathrooms. Old-fashioned breakfast room and pantry off the kitchen. $175,000.

5. There are _____ bedrooms.

6. There are _____ bathrooms.

7. The yard is large _____.

8. The house is cheap _____.

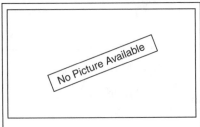

Spacious four-bedroom, two baths, city house is right in the center of action right on the boulevard. Small yard easy to maintain with a pool. $250,000.

9. The house is large _____.

10. There are _____ bathrooms.

11. The yard is _____ small.

12. The street is _____ busy for kids.

13. The house is _____ expensive.

 EXERCISE 2   *(Focus 2, page 140)*

Penelope Picky is having an elegant party this weekend. She's spending all day preparing for the party, but she's very hard to satisfy.

Complete the sentences with *too*, *enough*, or *not enough*, as necessary. The illustrations will help you create meaningful answers. Before you begin, look at the illustrations and review the word list.

The word list may help you, but don't limit yourself to those words. There are different ways to make meaningful responses for this exercise. Compare your answers with a partner's.

softly	toppings	weird	silly
rich	space	stylish	sexy
elegantly	loudly	spots	tight
long	fattening	money	sweet
light	wildly	large	time
quietly	seriously	cold	
loose	sophisticated	short	

AT THE CATERER'S

Example: **Caterer:** *What would you like to serve for dessert, madam? Cheesecake?*

Penelope: *No, cheesecake is too fattening, and you never serve enough.*

1.   **Caterer:** Ice cream?

     Penelope: No, _____

2.   **Caterer:** Chocolate mousse?

     Penelope: No, _____

3.   **Caterer:** Pastries?

     Penelope: No, _____

     Caterer: Flan?

     Penelope: Yes, that would be perfect. It's not too sweet, and it will be elegant enough.

AT THE DEPARTMENT STORE BUYING A DRESS FOR THE PARTY

4. **Salesclerk:** What about this short dress?

   Penelope: No, _____

5. **Salesclerk:** Perhaps you would prefer this elegant long dress?

   Penelope: No, _____

6. **Salesclerk:** What about this leopard skin print?

   Penelope: Definitely not, _____

7. **Salesclerk:** How about this one?

   Penelope: Yes, _____

AUDITIONING MUSICIANS FOR THE PARTY

8.   **Agent:** What about a rock band?

   Penelope: No, _____

9.   **Agent:** A string quartet?

   Penelope: No, _____

10.   **Agent:** I know a great country and western band.

    Penelope: No, _____

11.   **Agent:** What about a jazz quartet?

    Penelope: Perfect, _____

■ **EXERCISE 3**   *(Focus 3, page 142)*

Complete the following story by filling in each blank with *too much, too many, too little,* or *too few,* as appropriate.

Robin Bird: Good evening, folks. This is Robin Bird with another fascinating episode of *Lifestyles of the Extremely Rich*. We're here today with Ms. Mercedes Benz at her fabulous home, San Coupe, in California. Thanks for having us.

Mercedes: Certainly, Robin.

Robin: Mercedes, do you really have 12 bathrooms here at San Coupe?

Mercedes: Well, yes, Robin. I do have 12 bathrooms. Do you think that's (1) _____ bathrooms?

Robin: No, of course not. But it must take quite a few servants to keep all those bathrooms clean.

Mercedes: You're right, I never have enough servants. There are always (2) _____ servants around, and it takes (3) _____ energy to manage all of them, but I get by somehow.

Robin: Let's talk about the grounds surrounding San Coupe. How much land do you own?

Mercedes: Well, I'm just not sure how much land I own, but I know I have (4) _____ grass to mow in one day, and I have three swimming pools. Unfortunately, I don't get enough exercise because I just bought two new cars, and now I have (5) _____ time to do much swimming.

Robin: How many cars do you own now?

Mercedes: Seven, one for each day of the week. Of course, now I have the problem of (6) _____ garage space. But that's what happens when you have (7) _____ cars.

Robin: Can you believe that, folks? Seven cars! Well, we have to go, but Mercedes, I want to thank you very much for sharing San Coupe with us. I hope we didn't take up (8) _____ of your time.

Mercedes: It was my pleasure, Robin. A woman like me can never get (9) _____ publicity. I get (10) _____ opportunities to show off San Coupe.

■ EXERCISE 4   *(Focus 4, page 143)*

Write 5 statements that describe things you like about where you live now. Then write 5 statements describing things you don't like. Be sure to use *too* and *very* in your description. Share your list with a partner.

Example: *My apartment has too few rooms.*
My living room is very sunny.

THINGS I LIKE

1. _____
2. _____
3. _____
4. _____
5. _____

THINGS I DON'T LIKE

1. _____
2. _____
3. _____
4. _____
5. _____

Choose the word or phrase (*a, b, c,* or *d*) that best completes each sentence. Then circle the letter.

1. Thai food is hotter than Japanese food; by *hotter*, I mean _____ .

   a. as spicy

   b. less spicy

   c. spicier

   d. a little spicy

2. It's _____ for people who don't like spicy food.

   a. as hot

   b. hot enough

   c. hotter

   d. too hot

3. It can be spicy hot like Indian food, but _____ as Indian food.

   a. not greasy

   b. less greasy

   c. more greasy

   d. not as greasy

4. Thai cuisine is _____ and more exotic than heavy French food.

   a. as light

   b. less light

   c. lighter

   d. more light

5. Like the French chefs, Thai cooks use _____ fresh herbs and spices.

   a. enough

   b. many

   c. too few

   d. too many

6. *Sateh* is one of my favorite Thai dishes. It consists of meat served with a wonderful peanut sauce. You can make the sauce at home or buy _____ of the sauce at a gourmet shop.

   a. a clove

   b. a bottle

   c. a box

   d. a scoop

7. *Sateh* was originally Indonesian, but the Indonesian dish isn't _____ as the *sateh* from Thailand.

   a. as spicy

   b. less spicy

   c. quite spicy

   d. spicier

8–9. In my opinion, of _____ the world's cuisines, Asian cooking is _____ .

   a. a couple of

   b. none of

   c. all

   d. few

   a. delicious

   b. more delicious

   c. most delicious

   d. the most delicious

10. Roy had a heart attack last year. Before then, he never worried _____ about his health. His doctor told him to change his lifestyle, and gave him a diet and exercise plan.

    a. too little   c. very much

    b. enough   d. a great deal of

11–12. In order to have a more healthful diet, Roy started to eat _____ fruits and vegetables and _____ fat.

    a. fewer … less   c. some … much

    b. more … more   d. more … less

13–14. Instead of eating a _____ of chocolate when he wanted something sweet, Roy learned to eat an apple or a _____ of grapes.

    a. cup   a. bunch

    b. bar   b. dozen

    c. clove   c. leaf

    d. tablet   d. scoop

15–16. Before his heart attack, he ate _____ fast food, and he almost never ate _____ fresh fruits and vegetables.

    a. many   a. more

    b. a lot of   b. very much

    c. enough   c. a few

    d. too little   d. very many

EDITING PRACTICE

Questions 17–31: Circle the *one* underlined word or phrase that must be changed for the sentence to be grammatically correct.

17. Before his heart attack, Roy's diet wasn't (a) <u>as</u> healthy (b) <u>as</u> it is now. He ate (c) <u>alot</u> of salty and fried food, and he didn't eat (d) <u>very much</u> healthy food.

18. He still eats dessert, but now he has a (a) <u>bowl</u> of frozen yogurt instead of a (b) <u>few</u> (c) <u>scoops</u> of ice cream. Frozen yogurt doesn't have as much fat (d) <u>than</u> ice cream.

19. He has a much (a) <u>better</u> lifestyle now. In addition to a (b) <u>healthyer</u> diet, he's getting (c) <u>more</u> exercise, and he's smoking a lot (d) <u>less</u>.

20. It's been one year since Roy's heart attack, and he feels (a) <u>much</u> better (b) <u>than</u> he did before. He quit smoking, lost (c) <u>too much</u> weight, and continues to exercise (d) <u>a lot</u>.

21. Roy's family is (a) <u>very</u> happy—they love him (b) <u>too</u> much and are glad that he's taking (c) <u>better</u> care of himself (d) <u>than</u> he did before his heart attack.

22. He's also not under (a) <u>as much</u> stress as before; he quit his job because it was (b) <u>too</u> stressful (c) <u>for</u> him—and he's a lot (d) <u>more</u> happier now.

23. His doctor says that if he continues to do as well (a) <u>as</u> he's doing now, the risk of having another heart attack will be (b) <u>much</u> (c) <u>less</u>, and Roy will live a lot (d) <u>more long</u>.

24. I think North American food is (a) <u>less</u> interesting than other cuisines; it's one of (b) <u>the</u> (c) <u>blander</u>, (d) <u>least</u> imaginative cuisines that I know.

25. It uses too (a) <u>little</u> spices and fresh (b) <u>herbs</u> and (c) <u>too</u> (d) <u>many</u> canned and frozen ingredients.

26. Other cooking around the world uses a (a) <u>much</u> (b) <u>wider</u> variety of herbs and spices, so their food has (c) <u>more</u> flavor than (d) <u>we do</u>.

27. North Americans eat a lot of processed and frozen food, which has chemicals and is (a) <u>not</u> (b) <u>as healthful</u> (c) <u>than</u> diets with (d) <u>more</u> fresh, natural foods.

28. We also eat at fast-food restaurants, which serve greasy food with (a) <u>a lot</u> of calories. That's part of the reason that North Americans are much (b) <u>fatter</u> and (c) <u>less</u> healthy (d) <u>that</u> people of other nationalities.

29. (a) <u>Not all</u> North Americans eat fast food; some enjoy trying international food (b) <u>very much</u>, but to prepare that food at home isn't (c) <u>enough convenient</u> (d) <u>for them</u>.

30. Yes, (a) <u>some</u> have started to change their attitude about food, but (b) <u>no enough</u>—the average North American still eats (c) <u>too many</u> mashed potatoes and (d) <u>too much</u> beef.

31. If North Americans borrowed (a) <u>more</u> ideas from the cuisines of their various ethnic communities, they could learn (b) <u>a great deal</u> and have one of (c) <u>a</u> (d) <u>most</u> fascinating cooking in the world.

GIVING ADVICE AND EXPRESSING OPINIONS

Should, Ought To, Need To, Must, Had Better, Could, and Might

 EXERCISE 1   *(Focus 1, page 152)*

Advice columns appear in most North American newspapers. Readers write and ask for advice about their problems. Write four sentences of advice to the following people who are having problems. Use *should*, *should not*, or *ought to*. The first sentence has been done for you as an example.

ASK GABBY

> Dear Gabby,
>
>   I moved to Canada from Korea three years ago. My mom says I don't act Korean anymore. She thinks I'm acting too much like a Canadian because I like playing hockey with my friends. I'm not trying to be disrespectful to my mom. I just want to be like the other kids. What should I do?
>
>   Sincerely,
>   On Thin Ice

1. <u>First, you ought to talk to your mother.</u> _____

   _____

2. _____

   _____

3. _____

   _____

4. _____

   _____

Dear Gabby,

   I work all day as a cashier in a department store. When I come home, my husband expects me to make his dinner and clean the house. Not only that, but my husband is a slob. When he comes home from work, he leaves his clothes all over and then just watches TV. What should I do?

                                                      Sincerely,
                                                      Worn Out in Waukegan

1. _____
   _____
2. _____
   _____
3. _____
   _____
4. _____
   _____

Dear Gabby,

   I'm a 25-year-old construction worker. I am very dissatisfied with my job. I've always wanted to help people. I'd like to study nursing, but all my friends say nursing is women's work. What should I do?

                                                      Sincerely,
                                                      Dissatisfied in Dallas

1. _____
   _____
2. _____
   _____
3. _____
   _____
4. _____
   _____

EXERCISE 2 *(Focus 2, page 153)*

For each of the following situations, use the modal verbs in parentheses to give advice to the person who is trying to learn English.

Example: *Lori can't remember new vocabulary words.*
(need to) She needs to know the words to speak English well.
(should) She should study new words an hour every day.

Matthew can't understand movies in English.

1. (ought to) _____

2. (shouldn't) _____

Bill gets nervous when he speaks English.

3. (need to) _____

4. (should) _____

Kristi sometimes gets headaches when she speaks English too long.

5. (ought to) _____

6. (doesn't need to) _____

Geraldine makes a lot of spelling mistakes in English.

7. (need to) _____

8. (should) _____

David falls asleep in class.

9. (need to) _____

10. (shouldn't) _____

EXERCISE 3 *(Focus 3, page 154)*

Rosario wants to be a doctor. Complete the following sentences about Rosario, using *should,* *shouldn't*, *must*, or *must not*, as appropriate. Compare your answers with a partner. Explain why the answers you chose are most appropriate.

Example: *She should find out about medical schools.*

1. She _____ get high grades in college.

2. She _____ like biology.

3. She _____ study for seven years.

4. She _____ find some friends who also want to be doctors so they can support each other and study together.

5. She _____ apply for a scholarship.

6. She ＿＿＿＿＿＿ be afraid of blood.

7. She ＿＿＿＿＿＿ like to help people.

8. She ＿＿＿＿＿＿ be able to work long hours.

9. She ＿＿＿＿＿＿ work well under pressure.

10. She ＿＿＿＿＿＿ learn about different medicines.

■ EXERCISE 4 *(Focus 4, page 155)*

Complete the following sentences with *should, ought to, had better*, or their negative forms.

Example: *Mother to daughter:* You ___had better___ *wear a warm jacket, or you'll catch cold.*

1. **At a train station:** You ＿＿＿＿＿＿ buy your ticket. The train will be here in five minutes.

2. **Parent to child:** You ＿＿＿＿＿＿ eat your vegetables, or you won't get any dessert.

3. **Teacher to student:** You ＿＿＿＿＿＿ worry about this test. You'll do fine if you study. You got an A on all your other tests.

4. **One student to another:** I agree we ＿＿＿＿＿＿ study, but I'm ready for a break.

5. **Boss to worker:** You ＿＿＿＿＿＿ be late to work any more. If you come late again, you'll lose your job.

6. **Worker to coworker:** Quick, we ＿＿＿＿＿＿ look busy; the boss is coming.

7. **Worker to coworker:** You ＿＿＿＿＿＿ wear a tie to work if you want to impress the boss.

8. **Travel agent to tourist:** You ＿＿＿＿＿＿ leave home early, or you'll miss your flight because there is a lot of traffic at that time.

9. **At the airport:** You ＿＿＿＿＿＿ visit the pyramids while you are in Egypt. It's the chance of a lifetime!

10. **Police officer to driver:** You ＿＿＿＿＿＿ not drive so fast, or you will get another speeding ticket.

For each of the following pairs, write a sentence using *should, ought to, had better*, or their negative forms.

1. **Father to son:** ＿＿＿＿＿＿＿＿＿＿＿＿＿＿＿＿

＿＿＿＿＿＿＿＿＿＿＿＿＿＿＿＿＿＿＿＿

2. **Student to teacher:** ＿＿＿＿＿＿＿＿＿＿＿＿＿＿

＿＿＿＿＿＿＿＿＿＿＿＿＿＿＿＿＿＿＿＿

3. **Doctor to patient:** ＿＿＿＿＿＿＿＿＿＿＿＿＿＿

＿＿＿＿＿＿＿＿＿＿＿＿＿＿＿＿＿＿＿＿

4. **Mechanic to car owner:** ＿＿＿＿＿＿＿＿＿＿＿

＿＿＿＿＿＿＿＿＿＿＿＿＿＿＿＿＿＿＿＿

It is the week before final exams, and Victoria and Migalie are trying to decide what they are going to do today. Complete the following dialogue using *should*, *could*, or *might*, as appropriate. The first one has been done for you as an example.

Victoria: We _____should_____ study for the biology exam.

Migalie: I know we _____, but it's such a beautiful day. Why don't we go to the beach? We _____ invite those cute guys who live in the next dorm.

Victoria: Sure, and we _____ go swimming.

Migalie: Yeah, we _____ play volleyball and get a great tan.

Victoria: I know—we _____ get some hamburgers and have a barbecue!

Migalie: But if we go to the beach, I _____ buy a new bathing suit because mine is getting old.

Victoria: Okay, you get a new bathing suit, and I'll get the food.

Migalie: Well, if we're going to invite those guys, you _____ get some burgers.

Victoria: You're right. We also _____ buy some picnic supplies.

Migalie: Wait, do you have any money?

Victoria: I don't have very much.

Migalie: I _____ not have enough, either.

Victoria: So, what _____ we do?

Migalie: We _____ study for the biology exam.

■ **EXERCISE 6** *(Focus 6, page 160)*

For each of the following situations, use *might*, *could*, *should*, *ought to*, *need to*, *had better*, *must*, or their negative forms to give advice. There are many possible answers to each situation. Explain why you chose the modal verb for a situation. After you have completed the exercise, compare answers with a partner.

HISHAM IS GETTING A DRIVER'S LICENSE

Example: *have an accident*
He had better not have an accident while taking the road test.
Explanation: If he has an accident while taking the road test, he will not get his driver's license. A strong modal verb is necessary.

1. bring a passport or birth certificate _____

_____

Explanation: _____

_____

2. fail the written test _____

_____

Explanation: _____

_____

3. be nervous _____

_____

Explanation: _____

_____

4. practice parallel parking _____

_____

Explanation: _____

_____

ANGELICA IS REGISTERING FOR COLLEGE CLASSES

5. get her advisor's signature _____

_____

Explanation: _____

_____

6. register early _____

_____

Explanation: _____

_____

7. find out about the instructors _____

_____

Explanation: _____

_____

8. buy her books before classes start _____

_____

Explanation: _____

_____

IT'S MY MOTHER'S BIRTHDAY

9. buy her a card and gift _____
   _____

   Explanation: _____
   _____

10. bake a cake _____
   _____

   Explanation: _____
   _____

11. remind my father _____
   _____

   Explanation: _____
   _____

BEN AND SARAH ARE WRITING RESEARCH PAPERS

12. start researching early _____
   _____

   Explanation: _____
   _____
   _____

13. turn in the paper late _____
   _____

   Explanation: _____
   _____
   _____

14. look up information on the Internet
   _____

   Explanation: _____
   _____

15. go to the library _____
   _____

   Explanation: _____
   _____

DIEGO IS GETTING SICK

16. call the doctor _____

_____

Explanation: _____

_____

17. go to bed _____

_____

Explanation: _____

_____

18. take some aspirin _____

_____

Explanation: _____

_____

■ EXERCISE 7   (Focus 7, page 161)

Do you agree or disagree with the following statements? Check (✓) the appropriate column.

	Agree	Disagree
1. Men should help with the housework.	_____	_____
2. Women should not work outside the home.	_____	_____
3. Women should not be totally responsible for the child care.	_____	_____
4. Husbands ought to help their wives with the dishes.	_____	_____
5. Men and women should keep their traditional roles.	_____	_____
6. Boys shouldn't learn how to cook.	_____	_____
7. A college education ought to be available for both men and women.	_____	_____
8. Women should be encouraged to participate in athletics.	_____	_____
9. Wives ought to serve their husbands before they eat their own food.	_____	_____
10. A father should not help change the baby's diapers.	_____	_____
11. Women should learn how to change a tire.	_____	_____

EXERCISE 8   *(Focus 7, page 161)*

Compare your answers from Exercise 7 with your classmates'. Discuss your opinions.

EXERCISE 9   *(Focus 7, page 161)*

Use *should*, *ought to*, or their negative forms and the cues below to express your opinions. Then compare your opinions with a partner.

Example: *Men/help take care of children*
Men ought to help take care of children.

1. Women with small children/work outside the home

   _____

   _____

2. Men/wash clothes

   _____

   _____

3. Boys/learn how to sew

   _____

   _____

4. Girls/learn how to repair cars

   _____

   _____

5. Boys and girls/go to school together

   _____

   _____

6. Women/participate in the Olympic Games

   _____

   _____

7. Women/become doctors

   _____

   _____

8. Teenagers/be able to drink alcohol

   _____

   _____

9. Students/study all the time

   _____

   _____

MODALS OF NECESSITY AND PROHIBITION
Have To, Have Got To, Do Not Have To, Must/Must Not, Cannot

■ EXERCISE 1   *(Focus 1, page 168)*

Put a check mark (✓) by the sentences that are true.

____ 1. Before leaving on a trip abroad (to another country), you should get a travel book with information about that country.

____ 2. You shouldn't carry all of your money in cash, and you shouldn't put all your money in one place.

____ 3. To enter some tropical countries, you mustn't have some vaccinations and other shots to protect against tropical diseases.

____ 4. When you check in at the airport, you don't have to pay extra if you have too much luggage.

____ 5. You've got to pack your camera and passport in your suitcase.

____ 6. During nearly all international flights, you mustn't smoke.

____ 7. When traveling abroad, you must learn to say *please* and *thank you* in the local language.

____ 8. To drive in most countries, you have to have a driver's license.

____ 9. If you're a smart traveler, you should be able to carry all of your luggage by yourself.

____ 10. When you're in a North American city, you mustn't ask about neighborhoods that you should avoid (not go near).

____ 11. If you're lost in North America and you see a police officer, you should ask him/her for help.

____ 12. You can't bring plants or animals into Canada or the United States from another country.

■ EXERCISE 2   *(Focus 2, page 169)*

Complete the following conversation with the correct form of *must*, *have to*, or *have got to*, as indicated. When not indicated, answer with the pronoun and the auxiliary *do*. The first one has been done for you.

Claudia and Andres, two foreign tourists, are renting a car. They're asking the agent about driving in the United States.

Andres: ___Do I have to___ have a driver's license? (I + have to)

Agent: Yes, (1) _____.

Andres: What about Claudia? She has an international driver's license. (2) _____ get another license? (she + have to)

Agent: No, (3) _____. She can drive here with an international license.

Claudia: What about seat belts? (4) _____ wear seat belts? (we + have to)

Agent: Yes, you (5) _____ wear seat belts. (must) It's the law in most states.

Andres: What (6) _____ do with that thing in the front seat of the car? (we + have to)

Agent: What thing? (Andres points to the litter basket.) Oh, that's the litter basket. It's for litter: garbage, paper and things that you want to throw away.

Claudia: Can't we just throw it out the window?

Agent: No, you (7) _____ throw it out the window. (must + negative) There's a $500 fine for littering! You (8) _____ keep everything inside the car. (have got to)

Andres: (9) _____ drive on the left side of the road the way they do in England? (we + have to)

Agent: No!! You (10) _____ drive on the left. (must + negative) Stay on the right.

Claudia: Are there any other laws that we should know about?

Agent: Well, if you're going to turn right or left, you (11) _____ use your turn signal. (have to) On the highway, you (12) _____ follow the speed limit, and if you're driving more slowly than the other cars, you (13) _____ stay in the right lane. (must, have to) The left lane is for faster traffic. Obey the laws, or the police will stop you.

▪ EXERCISE 3   *(Focus 3, page 172)*

Fill in the blanks below with *have to* or *have got to*, whichever you think is more appropriate. The first one is done for you.

1. It's time for my yearly checkup. I ___have to___ remember to call the doctor's office sometime this month.

2. I burned my finger while I was cooking. The first-aid book says that I _____ hold my finger under cold water.

3. She spilled hot oil all over her leg and foot. John _____ take her to the emergency room, now!

4. What _____ (Irene) do for her first-aid class? She _____ practice CPR (Cardiopulmonary Resuscitation).

5. His face is blue! We _____ check his throat to see what he's choking on.

6. There are jellyfish in the area. The lifeguard's telling Tommy that he _____ stay out of the water today.

7. Did that little boy drown? He stopped breathing. The lifeguard _____ start mouth-to-mouth respiration as soon as possible.

8. I cut my finger, and it's bleeding a little. What should I do? The neighbor, who's a nurse, says that you _____ wash the cut, and then put a bandage on it.

9. There's something in my eye again! Oh, Lisa. You _____ stop wearing so much eye makeup.

10. The children _____ get their vaccinations before school starts.

Some children are at a swimming pool with their grandmother. The lifeguard is shouting at the children, but they're not paying any attention. Their grandmother is repeating the lifeguard's instructions. In the spaces below, write what she says, using *cannot (can't)* or *must not (mustn't)*. The first one is done for you.

1. Walk! No running!

   <u>You mustn't run! or You must not run.</u>

2. No diving in the shallow* water!

   _____

3. You're not allowed to go in the deep water until you pass a swimming test.

   _____

4. Don't take beach balls in the pool.

   _____

5. No pushing!

   _____

6. Get that radio away from the pool. No radios in the pool area!

   _____

7. Obey the rules! Stop breaking the rules!

   _____

8. Get that dog out of here! No pets allowed!

   _____

9. No eating or drinking in the pool area!

   _____

10. Stop hitting that little boy!

    _____

* *shallow:* not deep

Look at the chart below on North American etiquette, and complete the sentences using *have to*, *don't have to*, *cannot*, and *must not*. The first one is done for you.

NORTH AMERICAN ETIQUETTE

	Personal Hygiene	Introductions	
		Formal	Informal
Necessary	use deodorant wear clean clothes daily	smile shake hands say "Nice to meet you."	smile say "Hello"
Not Necessary	wear perfume, cologne	be very serious	shake hands
Prohibited	use too much perfume, makeup	kiss, hug	kiss, hug

	Tipping	Table Manners	Clothing
Necessary	leave the waiter/waitress a 15 percent tip	wait to eat until everyone is served	wear conservative clothes in business/law/religious services
Not Necessary	tip bad waiter/waitress leave a tip in a fast-food restaurant	accept offers of food	wear conservative clothes in other situations
Prohibited	tip government officials (e.g., police, customs)	make noise with mouth when eating	go barefoot* (except at the beach)

* *go barefoot:* not wear shoes
(Some information from *Culturgram - United States of America*, Brigham Young University, David M. Kennedy Center for International Studies, 1985)

1. When you meet someone at a classmate's party, you <u>don't have to</u> shake hands.

2. North Americans don't have a lot of physical contact with each other, especially with strangers. When you meet someone for the first time, you _____ kiss or hug.

3. To make a good impression at a job interview, you _____ dress conservatively, and you _____ put on too much perfume.

4. North Americans like a good sense of humor. Even in business, a person _____ be formal and serious all the time.

5. For satisfactory service in a restaurant, it is customary to leave a 15 percent tip, but if the service is poor, you _____ tip the waiter that much.

6. To be accepted in North American society, you _____ take a bath every day, use deodorant, and wear clean clothes.

7. You _____ go barefoot to a church, mosque, synagogue, or temple.

8. A business executive _____ shake hands when he meets someone for the first time.

9. On most college and university campuses, a student _____ dress up for classes; in fact, it's very casual.

10. Direct eye contact is important for North Americans. You _____ look at them directly and smile when you meet them, or they might think you're dishonest.

Using the chart from Exercise 5 as a guide, write your own sentences about customs in your family's native country. Use *have to*, *don't have to*, *cannot*, and *must not*.

NECESSARY

1. _____

   _____

2. _____

   _____

3. _____

   _____

NOT NECESSARY

4. _____

   _____

5. _____

   _____

6. _____

   _____

PROHIBITED

7. _____

   _____

8. _____

   _____

9. _____

   _____

Using the information from the chart in Exercise 5, complete the following conversation about María's trip to North America. Use *must*, *have to*, or *don't have to*, in the present, past, or future. The first one is done for you.

José: María, how was your trip to America? You were there all summer, right?

María: Yes, I went there with an exchange program. I stayed with a family. It was great!

José: What was it like? Is it true that Americans ____have to____ take two showers a day or they don't feel clean?

María: No, that's not true.

José: Is it true that they are informal?

María: Yes, while I was there, I (1) _____ wear a dress or a skirt. Every day I wore shorts and sneakers, except one day when we went to court. The father of the family is a lawyer, and he says that in a courtroom, you (2) _____ dress more formally.

José: How was the food? Is it true that they eat hamburgers and hot dogs every day?

María: No, that's not true, but in the morning I (3) _____ eat cereal and drink American coffee.

José: Was it safe to drink the water, or (4) _____ boil the water before drinking it?

María: The water was very safe to drink.

José: Was the family rich?

María: No, they were middle class. They didn't have servants, so I (5) _____ help around the house. I (6) _____ clean my own room and help with the dishes. There was yard work, too, but I (7) _____ help with that.

José: What else (8) _____ do?

María: I (9) _____ walk the dog.

José: Is it true that in North America you (10) _____ treat pets almost like people?

María: Yes, the dog was a member of the family. The mother of the family said to me, "María, dogs are our friends. We (11) _____ love and respect them."

José: How about the people? Is it true that the people are nice?

María: Oh, yes! But one time I'm afraid that I offended some friends of the family. I asked a woman about her salary. The family told me, "Mary, you (12) _____ ask about a person's salary, age, or weight. It's too personal."

José: I'd like to go next summer. What (13) _____ do?

María: Well, first, you (14) _____ get an application form and fill it out. I can help you.

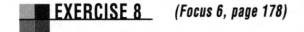

EXERCISE 8   *(Focus 6, page 178)*

PAIR/INDIVIDUAL/GROUP

Exchange your answers to Exercise 6 with a classmate's (preferably someone from a different country and culture). Now imagine that you are planning a trip to that person's hometown. Write sentences about your plans, using *have to/don't have to*, *will have to/won't have to*, or *must*. Share your answers with the class.

NECESSARY

1. _____
   _____

2. _____
   _____

3. _____
   _____

NOT NECESSARY

4. _____
   _____

5. _____
   _____

6. _____
   _____

PROHIBITED

7. _____
   _____

8. _____
   _____

9. _____
   _____

EXPRESSING LIKES AND DISLIKES

EXERCISE 1   *(Focus 1, page 186)*

The students in Glenda's class have a lot in common. Complete the following sentences about them, using *too* or *either*.

Example: *Her son doesn't eat vegetables, and my daughter doesn't either.*

1. Ramón studies math, and María José _____
2. I don't understand Greek, and my friends _____
3. Ann doesn't like liver, and her sister _____
4. Cheryl loves animals, and her children _____
5. Elizabeth loves the English language, and my students _____
6. Lee doesn't like to write in English, and Dora _____
7. Kim listens to classical music, and I _____
8. She doesn't listen to hip-hop, and I _____
9. I like the teacher's new haircut, and the other students _____
10. So Young doesn't like it, and Hyung Gue _____

EXERCISE 2   *(Focus 2, page 186)*

Copy the sentences from Exercise 1, changing *too* and *either* to *so* and *neither*.

Example: *Her son doesn't eat vegetables, and neither does my daughter.*

1. _____
2. _____
3. _____
4. _____
5. _____
6. _____
7. _____
8. _____
9. _____
10. _____

Correct the mistakes in the following sentences.

1. Scott lives in Iowa, and so is Debbie.

2. I don't know how to windsurf, and my brother doesn't neither.

3. Sung can't type and neither Fathi can.

4. Mark went to the wrong restaurant, and so didn't Alonzo.

5. Bob didn't go sailing, and either did Irene.

6. Mayumi hasn't been here long, and Sato isn't either.

7. Cynthia was in class yesterday, and you was too.

8. You were sick last week, and so wasn't Sheila.

9. Lee won't come with us, and either will Kim.

10. Maureen has a cute boyfriend, and so has Patty.

Read the following dialog between coworkers. Match the sentences in the first column with the appropriate short phrase in the second column. The first one is done for you.

1. Oliver went to the union meeting last night. _b_	a. I am too.
2. His boss wasn't there. ___	b. I did too.
3. My boss thinks everything is fine at work. ___	c. My boss, Mr. Fagin, does too.
4. He wasn't happy to hear about the meeting. ___	d. Mr. Fagin hasn't either.
5. He hasn't been acting very professional about this. ___	e. Mine wasn't either.
6. He got angry—I felt bad about what he said to us. ___	f. Neither does Mr. Fagin.
7. I think it's wrong not to say what you think. ___	g. Neither was Mr. Fagin!
8. Well, I'm for the union. ___	h. Neither will Mr. Fagin.
9. My boss doesn't like unions. ___	i. So can I!
10. My manager won't be happy if we vote for a union. ___	j. So did I.
11. This is a free country and Oliver can do what he wants. ___	k. So do I.

Complete the conversation below with short phrases showing agreement (*So do I / I don't either*) or hedges (*Kind of / Sort of*).

IN WRITING CLASS:

Brian: Did the teacher like your composition?

Daniel: Well, (1) _____.

Brian: What grade did you get?

Daniel: I got a C.

Brian: (2) _____. Actually, I'm happy. I don't usually pass.

Daniel: (3) _____. I'm terrible at writing. Conversation class is more fun. I'm better at speaking.

Brian: (4) _____. How about Reading? Do you like Reading class?

Daniel: (5) _____. I don't really like the teacher.

Brian: (6) _____.

Daniel: I'm tired of studying English.

Brian: (7) _____.

Daniel: I like my other classes a lot better.

Brian: What other classes?

Daniel: I'm taking music classes.

Brian: Really?! (8) _____! I'm taking Music Theory and guitar lessons. How about you?

Daniel: I'm taking Theory and voice lessons. Who's your Theory teacher?

Brian: Professor Kaplan.

Daniel: Do you like the class?

Brian: (9) _____. It's difficult. I like the other class better. Do you like your voice lessons?

Daniel: (10) _____. I like Music Theory better. It's my favorite class.

In Unit 7, there is an exercise on right- and left-brain preferences. The list below shows some additional characteristics of "right-brain" and "left-brain" people. Check (✓) the sentences that are true for you. Then add up the number of check marks in each column to see if you are left-brain dominant, right-brain dominant, or balanced. Are your results the same as before?

After you finish, put a circle around all of the gerunds in the lists, and underline the infinitives.

LEFT-BRAIN	RIGHT-BRAIN
____ I have a place for everything and a system for doing things.	____ I enjoy swimming.
____ I enjoy sewing.	____ I enjoy skiing.
____ I enjoy chess.	____ I enjoy bicycling.
____ I understand contracts, instruction manuals, and legal documents.	____ I am good at thinking up new ideas.
____ I like to plan and arrange the details of a trip.	____ I enjoy photography.
____ I like to collect things.	____ I can understand charts and diagrams.
____ I enjoy working on home improvements.	____ I like to relax and just do nothing.
____ I enjoy writing.	____ I enjoy dancing.
____ I play bridge.	____ I like to paint or sketch.
____ I like to read.	____ I postpone making telephone calls.
____ I play a musical instrument.	____ I enjoy fishing.
____ I enjoy doing crossword puzzles.	____ I enjoy running.
____ After meeting a person for the first time, I remember the person's name.	____ After meeting a person for the first time, I remember the person's face.
____ Before buying something, I read the label and compare prices.	____ When shopping, I buy what I like.
____ I'm good at speaking.	____ I like to sing in the shower.
____ I like competing with others.	____ I enjoy rearranging my furniture and decorating my home.
____ Total	____ Total

(From "Orientations Inventory," University Associates, The 1988 Annual: Developing Human Resources, PP. 60–63.)

Are you a left-brain person or a right-brain person? _____

How many gerunds did you circle? _____

How many infinitives did you underline? _____

Complete the following sentences. Use a gerund or infinitive in your answer.

Example: *I hate ironing.*

1. _____ is one of my hobbies.
2. I enjoy _____ and _____.
3. I love _____.
4. I hate _____.
5. I'm good at _____.
6. When I was a little boy/girl, _____ was something that I loved to do.
7. On my vacations, I like _____.
8. I feel good after I finish _____.
9. _____ is something I always postpone doing.
10. _____ and _____ are two Olympic sports.

■ **EXERCISE 8**   *(Focus 6, page 192)*

Working in groups of 3–4, compare your answers to Exercises 6 and 7. Take turns reading a statement about yourself. If you agree with someone, say *I* _____ *too, So* _____ *I, I* _____ *either*, or *Neither* _____ *I.*

_____

_____

_____

_____

_____

_____

Choose the word or phrase (*a, b, c,* or *d*) that best completes each sentence. Then circle the letter.

1. I don't like shopping, and Nancy _____.

   a. doesn't either   c. isn't either

   b. doesn't too   d. isn't neither

2. Bobby has a pair of skates, and _____.

   a. Irene has too   c. so does Irene

   b. Irene is too   d. so has Irene

3. Kelly _____ to go fishing, and so does Alex.

   a. does like   c. is like

   b. doesn't like   d. likes

4. Robin loved the movie, and _____.

   a. I loved too   c. so did I

   b. I didn't   d. so do I

5. Claire enjoys _____ antiques.

   a. collect   c. collecting

   b. collects   d. to collect

6. In North American classrooms, the students _____ stand when the teacher enters the room.

   a. don't have to   c. must not

   b. haven't got   d. should not

7. In some classes, students may eat, but they _____ smoke; it's the law.

   a. don't have to   c. mustn't

   b. haven't got   d. shouldn't

8. During class the teacher can have something to drink and the students _____.

   a. will, too   c. can, too

   b. are, too   d. drink, too

9. However, students _____ stand up and walk around the class while the teacher is talking.

   a. oughtn't to   c. shouldn't

   b. have got to   d. will have to

10. When I was a student, I _____ treat my teachers with more respect than students do nowadays.

    a. didn't have to   c. had to

    b. had got to   d. must have

11. _____ do anything to prevent heart disease?

    a. Have got I   c. Should I

    b. Ought I to   d. Had better I

12. The Heart Association gives some advice: you _____ eat healthy food, without too much fat or cholesterol.

    a. should   c. had better not

    b. must   d. could

13. If you don't want to die of heart disease, you _____ follow a low-fat diet, get more exercise, and get frequent check-ups from a doctor.

    a. shouldn't   c. could

    b. had better   d. had better not

14. If you feel chest pains, you _____ see a doctor as soon as possible, or your life may be in danger.

    a. could   c. must

    b. had better not   d. ought to

15. Finally, you _____ try to eliminate stress as much as possible from your everyday life.

    a. don't have to   c. couldn't

    b. shouldn't   d. should

EDITING PRACTICE

Questions 16-30: Circle the *one* underlined word or phrase that must be changed for the sentence to be grammatically correct.

16. Frank (a) <u>hasn't seen</u> that new movie about (b) <u>skiing</u>, and I (c) <u>haven't</u> (d) <u>neither</u>.

17. After he (a) <u>finish</u> (b) <u>washing</u> the dishes, Yared wants to go for a bike ride. (c) <u>So</u> (d) <u>do I</u>.

18. I (a) <u>can</u> understand why he loves (b) <u>working</u> with computers, and his mother (c) <u>can</u> (d) <u>either</u>.

19. Hilda enjoys (a) <u>to be</u> outside in her yard gardening, (b) <u>and</u> (c) <u>Florence does</u>, (d) <u>too</u>.

20. She stays in good physical shape by (a) <u>jogging</u> and (b) <u>to run</u>. (c) <u>So</u> (d) <u>does</u> her boyfriend.

21. I think that if a person lives in North America, he or she (a) <u>should</u> learn how to swim. When my (b) <u>parents</u> (c) <u>were</u> in college, they (d) <u>must to</u> pass a swimming test in order to graduate.

22. But at most colleges nowadays, a student (a) <u>doesn't</u> (b) <u>have</u> to do that as a requirement for graduation. You're right. I (c) <u>didn't</u> (d) <u>had to</u> do that when I was in college.

23. (a) <u>Ought I</u> learn to be safe around water? Yes, you (b) <u>should</u>. You (c) <u>ought to</u> take water safety classes from the Red Cross. The first rule in water safety is that you (d) <u>shouldn't</u> swim alone.

24. The second rule in water safety is that to save a drowning person, you (a) <u>mustn't</u> try to swim to him. You (b) <u>ought to</u> throw something, or you (c) <u>could</u> (d) <u>to reach</u> for the drowning person with something like a pole or towel.

25. Children (a) <u>should</u> (b) <u>learn</u> about water safety. They (c) <u>have got to</u> go near the water alone; an adult <u>should</u> always be with them.

26. (a) <u>I have</u> a toothache. (b) <u>What I should</u> do? Well, you (c) <u>could</u> take some aspirin, but it is probably (d) <u>better</u> to see the dentist.

27. I know I (a) <u>had better not</u> be afraid (b) <u>to go</u> to the dentist, but I always (c) <u>get nervous</u> sitting in the (d) <u>dentist's</u> chair.

28. The dentist (a) <u>makes</u> me feel anxious and (b) <u>so does his</u> assistant. Let me see what it (c) <u>looks</u> like. Oh, that tooth looks painful, and (d) <u>so the tooth</u> next to it.

29. You (a) <u>must</u> (b) <u>see</u> the dentist right away! To avoid painful toothaches, you (c) <u>could</u> brush your teeth and <u>use</u> dental floss.

30. You (a) <u>ought to</u> (b) <u>visit</u> a dentist twice a year and your children (c) <u>should</u> (d) <u>either</u>.

PRESENT PERFECT
Since and *For*

 EXERCISE 1   *(Focus 1, page 198)*

Below are some important events in the life of Carmen Alvarez. Decide whether each is a past event, a present event, or an event that began in the past and has continued to the present. Write the sentences under the correct category heading. The first one has been done for you as an example.

She has volunteered at the hospital since she moved to New Mexico.
She is studying at the University of New Mexico.
She wanted to be a doctor when she was a child.
She has studied at the University of New Mexico for three years.
She wants to be a doctor.
She moved to New Mexico.
She has wanted to be a doctor since she was a child.
She began studying at the University of New Mexico three years ago.
She is volunteering at the hospital.

PAST

1. _____
2. _____
3. _____

PRESENT

1. _____
2. _____
3. _____

BEGAN IN THE PAST AND CONTINUES NOW

1. <u>She has volunteered at the hospital since she moved to New Mexico.</u>
2. _____
3. _____

■ EXERCISE 2   *(Focus 1, page 198)*

Using Exercise 1 as a model, write sentences about events in your own life.

PAST

1. _____

2. _____

3. _____

PRESENT

1. _____

2. _____

3. _____

BEGAN IN THE PAST AND CONTINUES NOW

1. _____

2. _____

3. _____

■ EXERCISE 3   *(Focus 2, page 200)*

Before you can donate blood, you must answer several questions about your medical history. Complete the following dialogue between a blood donor and an interviewer, using the correct form of each verb in parentheses in the present perfect. The first one has been done for you.

Interviewer: How long ___has it been___ (it be) since you ate?

Donor: I _____ (not eat) anything since breakfast.

Interviewer: _____ (you give) blood before?

Donor: Yes, I _____ (give) blood many times.

Interviewer: Really? How long _____ (it be) since you last donated blood?

Donor: I _____ (not donate) blood for a year.

Interviewer: _____ (you have) any serious illnesses?

Donor: No, I _____ (not have) any illnesses.

Interviewer: _____ (you be) in the hospital in the past five years?

Donor: No, I _____ (not be) hospitalized.

Interviewer:	_____ (you travel) abroad?
Donor:	Yes, I _____ (go) to South America.
Interviewer:	How long ago was that?
Donor:	I was in South America in 2000, but I _____ (live) in the United States since then.
Interviewer:	Thanks for answering the questions. Now please roll up your sleeve.

■■ EXERCISE 4 *(Focus 2, page 200)*

Copy the interviewer's six questions from the previous exercise.

1. _____
2. _____
3. _____
4. _____
5. _____
6. _____

Take turns role-playing the interview with a partner. Answer the questions using your own experiences and history.

■■ EXERCISE 5 *(Focus 3, page 202)*

Complete the following dialogue by putting *since* or *for* in each blank. The blank in the sign in front of the castle has been filled in for you as an example.

Count Dracula:	Good evening, Mr. Stoker. Welcome to the Count Dracula Blood Blank. So nice of you to come. We would like to take your blood, but first we want to see if you're our type. Would you answer a few questions?
Stoker:	Well, uh, I guess so.
Count Dracula:	How long has it been _____ you arrived in Transylvania?
Stoker:	I just arrived. I've been here _____ only two hours.
Count Dracula:	Oh! Have you had time to explore the castle?
Stoker:	Well, I've walked around a little _____ I got here. The castle is interesting, but that back room is full of bats.
Count Dracula:	Yes, we've had that problem _____ the castle was built. That reminds me, how long has it been _____ you flew at night?
Stoker:	What? I haven't flown at night _____ last year. I'm afraid of the dark.

Count Dracula: Well, perhaps we can help you with that problem. How long has it been _____ you've been in a cemetery?

Stoker: These are the strangest questions I've ever heard. I guess the last time was in March. Yes, it's been three months _____ I was in a cemetery.

Count Dracula: Very good. Finally, Mr. Stoker, have you given blood before?

Stoker: Yes, but I haven't donated _____ at least six months.

Count Dracula: Wonderful! Because you've answered all our questions, we've decided you're a perfect victim—I mean candidate. Please roll down your collar.

■ EXERCISE 6   (Focus 4, page 203)

Look at the personnel file for Mercy Hospital. Which doctor has worked at the hospital the longest? Which nurse?

Use the information from the personnel files to make statements with the words given below.

Example: Dr. Zhivago / since *Dr. Zhivago has worked at Mercy hospital since 1973.*

1. Dr. Moreau / for _____
   _____

2. Dr. Jekyll / since _____
   _____

3. Dr. Zhivago and Nurse Nightingale / for
   _____

4. Dr. Faust / for _____
   _____

5. Nurse Ratchet / for _____
   _____

Doctors	First Year Employed	Nurses	First Year Employed
Dr. Doolittle	1973	Nurse Candystripe	1975
Dr. Faust	1981	Nurse Nightingale	1973
Dr. Freud	1988	Nurse Ratchet	1967
Dr. Jekyll	1978	Nurse Shark	1984
Dr. Livingston	1969		
Dr. Moreau	1958		
Dr. Spock	1988		
Dr. Zhivago	1973		

Mercy Hospital — Personnel File

23

6. Dr. Doolittle / since _____
   _____

7. Dr. Spock / for _____
   _____

8. Nurse Candystripe / for _____
   _____

9. Nurse Shark / since _____
   _____

10. Dr. Livingston / since _____

_____

11. Dr. Freud and Dr. Spock / since _____

_____

■ EXERCISE 7   (Focus 5, page 204)

Rewrite the sentences using the present perfect and *since* or *for*. Remember that the present perfect cannot be used with all verbs.

Example: She works at the hospital. She began working there six years ago.
She has worked at the hospital for six years.

1. Lisa started taking that medicine in 2004. She still takes it today.

_____

2. Do you want to be a surgeon? Did you want to be a surgeon when you were a child?

_____

3. Larry is an X-ray technician. He began this career in 1989.

_____

4. My stomach doesn't hurt anymore. It stopped hurting when I took the medication.

_____

5. Joe delivers flowers to the hospital every day. He began delivering flowers two years ago.

_____

6. Sylvia met my doctor. They met at a hospital fundraiser.

_____

7. It isn't raining; it stopped raining at 5:00.

_____

8. Doug arrived at the hospital 30 minutes ago. The doctor is still in the room with him.

_____

9. Medical technology was improving during the last century. It is still improving.

_____

10. She doesn't take that medicine anymore. She stopped taking that medicine when it made her sick.

_____

PRESENT PERFECT AND SIMPLE PAST
Ever and *Never, Already* and *Yet*

 EXERCISE 1   *(Focus 1, page 214)*

Decide if the following verbs should be in the simple past or the present perfect. Then circle the correct form.

Captain Michael Johnson, one of the best commercial airline pilots in the world, is retiring this year. He (1) began / has begun working for Western Airlines 35 years ago. In the beginning of his career, he (2) flew / has flown only domestic flights, but later on the company (3) told / has told him to fly internationally. Captain Mike, as the flight attendants call him, (4) flew / has flown around the world many times. He (5) met / has met a lot of people and (6) saw / has seen a lot of different places. In one year he (7) went / has gone to India, Egypt, and Greece, where he (8) saw / has seen the Taj Mahal, the pyramids, and the Acropolis. In addition, (9) he did / has done a lot of exciting things. On one trip, in 1980, he (10) jumped / has jumped from an airplane with a parachute, and on another trip he (11) rode / has ridden in a submarine. But his life (12) wasn't / hasn't been easy. In 1992 his plane almost (13) crashed / has crashed; he (14) had / has had to make an emergency landing. Ten years ago, he (15) had / has had cancer, but Captain Mike (16) fought / has fought the cancer and (17) won / has won. All in all, he (18) was / has been very lucky, and so (19) did / have we here at Western Airlines. We're going to miss you, Captain Mike.

Have you ever done these things? Using the words below and the present perfect, write questions and answers about your experiences. If you haven't ever done the activity, use *never* or *not + ever*.

Example: eat ants   *Have you ever eaten ants?*
                                Yes, I have.
                                OR *No, I haven't ever eaten ants. / No, I've never eaten ants.*

1. find a wallet in the street
   Q: _____
   A: _____

2. fly in a helicopter
   Q: _____
   A: _____

3. shoot a gun
   Q: _____
   A: _____

4. break a bone
   Q: _____
   A: _____

5. give blood
   Q: _____
   A: _____

6. meet a famous person
   Q: _____
   A: _____

7. have a car accident
   Q: _____
   A: _____

8. wear snowshoes
   Q: _____
   A: _____

9. ride a camel
   Q: _____
   A: _____

10. see a penguin
    Q: _____
    A: _____

Using the verbs from Exercise 2, ask a North American if he or she has ever done those activities. If he or she has, ask the appropriate questions about the activity (*When, where, . . .?*). Write all of the answers.

1. _____
   _____

2. _____
   _____

3. _____
   _____

4. _____
   _____

5. _____
   _____

6. _____
   _____

7. _____
   _____

8. _____
   _____

9. _____
   _____

10. _____
    _____

Sonia is going to take another trip abroad. Her friend, Nolan, is asking her questions about the trip. Using the words and pictures below, write Nolan's questions in the present perfect. Be careful—the verbs might need to be changed.

Example: already / you / camera /  / have / for / buy / your?

Have you already bought film for your camera?
No, I haven't.

1. buy / already / you / ticket / your /  / have?

_____

Yes, I have. That's the first thing I did.

2. a/an / ever / ticket / on / a / you / lose / have / trip / ?

_____

Yes, I have. On one trip someone stole my ticket.

3. reservations / have / already /  / you / your / make?

_____

No, I haven't. I never make any reservations.

4. check / forecast /  / have / out / the / you?

_____

Yes, I have. The weather's going to be nice and sunny.

5. you /  / yet / pack / your / have?

_____

No, I haven't done that yet. That's the last thing I do before a trip.

6. yet / you / a / / find / sitter / have?

_____

Yes, I have. My mother is going to take care of Tabby.

7. / already / your / get / you / have?

_____

Yes. I got it a long time ago.

8. already / for / you / visa /  / a / have?

_____

Yes, I have. I had to write to the consulate in Washington, D.C.

9. change / your / yet / you / have /  ?

_____

No, I haven't done that yet. I'm going to wait until I arrive.

10.  / you / read / have / yet / travel / any?

_____

Yes, I have. I went to the library a long time ago.

11. 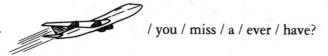 / you / miss / a / ever / have?

_____

No, I haven't. I've been very lucky.

12. someone / airport / ever / / else's / at / you / the / take / have?

_____

No, I haven't ever done that, but one time a man took mine.

EXERCISE 1 *(Focus 1, page 228 and Focus 2, page 229)*

Match the pictures with phrases from the list. Write sentences that give explanations for the situation using the present perfect progressive. Use "just" when appropriate. The first one has been done for you as an example.

lift boxes	sit in the sun	unpack dishes	move furniture	sleep
swim	move into new house	look for shells	~~have nightmares~~	dream

1. He has just been having a nightmare.

2. _____

3. _____

4. _____

5. _____

6. _____

7. _____

8. _____

9. _____

10. _____

EXERCISE 2 (Focus 2, page 229)

Look at the pictures in Exercise 1 and ask your partner questions about the pictures using the present perfect progressive.

Example: A: *What has he just been doing?*
B: *He's been having a nightmare.*

EXERCISE 3 (Focus 2, page 229)

Work in groups of three. Using the cues, ask one group member questions about what he or she has been doing since coming to class. Then tell the third group member. Take turns asking the questions and telling the person's answers to the third group member.

Example: speak only English
A: *Have you been speaking only English since you came to class?*
B: *Yes, I've been speaking only English.*
A: (to other group member) *She has been speaking only English.*

1. speak only English
2. talk to classmates
3. study grammar
4. do exercises
5. read in English
6. listen to the teacher
7. whisper to friends
8. sing in English
9. take notes

EXERCISE 4 (Focus 3, page 230)

Using the given time frame as a cue, think of an activity that you have been doing and continue to do today. Write a sentence for each. The first one has been done for you.

1. since last year
   I have been living on my own since last year.

2. since the beginning of the semester (quarter)

3. for the past week

4. since I started learning English

_____

5. for the past two years

_____

6. since my last birthday

_____

7. since last weekend

_____

8. since last winter

_____

9. for the past two weeks

_____

10. since last night

_____

■ EXERCISE 5   *(Focus 4, page 231)*

Fill in each blank with the appropriate form of the verb in parentheses. The first one has been done for you as an example.

Joel: Jimmy, you look terrible. What _have you been doing_ (you do) recently?

Jimmy: I _____ (not sleep) well lately.

Joel: _____ (you feel) sick?

Jimmy: I _____ (not feel) sick. My allergies _____ (bother) me for the past week or so.

Joel: _____ (something, happen) recently at school that is bothering you?

Jimmy: Well . . . not really.

Joel: What _____ (worry) you?

Jimmy: I _____ (think) about my grammar exam for the past couple of days.

Joel: Why?

Jimmy: We _____ (study) the present perfect progressive recently, and I'm not sure I understand it.

Joel: _____ (you study) hard and _____ (ask) for help when you need it?

Jimmy: Yes, I _____ (memorize) the form of the present perfect progressive, and I _____ (try) to use it whenever I speak English.

Joel: Sounds like you don't have anything to worry about. I'm sure you'll do fine.

List three changes you have been making in your life. Add a time phrase to show that the activity started recently.

Example: *Recently, I have been working late.*

1. _____

2. _____

3. _____

■ **EXERCISE 7**   *(Focus 5, page 232)*

Fill in each blank with the present perfect or present perfect progressive as appropriate. The first one has been done for you as an example.

For years I ____have read____ (read) a book right before I go to sleep. Recently, I (1) _____ (read) biographies. I read biographies of Charlie Chaplin and Mahatma Gandhi, and for the past couple of nights I (2) _____ (read) about Jane Addams.

I (3) _____ just _____ (realize) that Mom's sixtieth birthday is coming up soon, and it (4) _____ (be) a long time since we did something for her birthday. I think we should do something special this year.

What do you suggest?

Well, recently, I (5) _____ (collect) some pictures of us as children. I thought if we got some more pictures we could make a nice collection.

Mom used to get up at 6:30 every morning, but now she's on vacation, and she (6) _____ (wake up) at 7:30. It is only one hour, but it makes a big difference. She (7) _____ (have) more energy since she (8) _____ (be) on vacation.

George just returned from Japan. He (9) _____ (work) there for the past two months. Over the past year his company (10) _____ (set up) a new branch in Tokyo.

Choose the *one* word or phrase (*a, b, c,* or *d*) that best completes each sentence. Then circle the letter.

1. _____ to the Great Smokies National Park since it was improved?

   a. Have you been gone

   b. Did you went

   c. Have you gone

   d. Did you go

2. No, but I _____ to go there next summer.

   a. has wanted

   b. have been

   c. wants

   d. want

3. I _____ there; I returned last night.

   a. have just been camping

   b. have been camping there just

   c. just have been camping

   d. have camped

4. I _____ in such a beautiful park since I was in Yellowstone National Park.

   a. no stayed

   b. haven't stayed

   c. haven't staied

   d. don't stay

5. The forest and mountains are beautiful, but the campsites are rough. They _____ all the comforts of home.

   a. haven't had

   b. hadn't

   c. don't have

   d. haven't

6. How _____ the park?

   a. have they improved

   b. they have been improving

   c. they have improved

   d. have they been improved

7. Recently, the Park Service _____ more campsites.

   a. have added

   b. has been adding

   c. is adding

   d. have been adding

8. For many years, the park rangers _____ more hiking trails.

   a. has developed

   b. have been developed

   c. developed

   d. have been developing

9. Rangers have protected the natural beauty of the Great Smokies National Park _____ it was created.

   a. for

   b. when

   c. since

   d. that

10. In the past 30 years, computers _____ an important part of everyday life.

   a. have become
   b. has become
   c. have became
   d. have becomed

11. We _____ computers move into the workplace, schools, and homes since the invention of the microchip.

   a. have saw
   b. have seed
   c. have been seeing
   d. have seen

12. _____ computers have become more important, it has become more important to be computer literate.

   a. When
   b. Since
   c. For
   d. At the time

13. Almost every part of our lives _____ computerized over the past three decades.

   a. have been
   b. has been
   c. has been doing
   d. have been doing

14. Since I _____ in high school, I _____ a computer and the Internet to help me with my assignments.

   a. 've been being . . . 've been using
   b. was . . . 've used
   c. 've been . . . 've been using
   d. 've been . . . used

15. Yesterday, I _____ research on the Internet.

   a. have done
   b. did
   c. has done
   d. have been doing

EDITING PRACTICE

Questions 16–32: Identify the *one* underlined word or phrase that must be changed for the sentence to be grammatically correct.

16. Where (a) have you (b) been? I (c) have (d) seen not you around here lately.

17. (a) I've (b) just (c) been visiting my brother (d) since the past two weeks. He lives in Anchorage, Alaska.

18. Anchorage, Alaska? Why (a) were you (b) visiting Anchorage in the middle of the winter? What (c) have you (d) be doing there for two weeks?

19. Winter in Alaska is fun. I (a) have been (b) skiing and ice (c) skating. Also I (d) seen a dog sled race.

20. (a) Have you (b) never (c) seen a dog sled race? No, I (d) haven't.

21. The native people of Northern Canada and Alaska (a) have (b) been (c) participating in dog sled races (d) since more than 500 years.

22. I found out that the Inuit people (a) has (b) been using dog sleds as their main method of transportation (c) since they (d) settled in North America.

23. The dogs (a) <u>have</u> (b) <u>pulled</u> sleds during the winter for hundreds of years. They (c) <u>have</u> (d) <u>carryed</u> people and equipment across the frozen land.

24. (a) <u>In the past</u>, every Inuit family (b) <u>has been having</u> a dog sled team because it (c) <u>was</u> (d) <u>their</u> only source of transportation.

25. (a) <u>Since</u> the invention of the snowmobile, dog sleds (b) <u>has</u> (c) <u>become</u> less popular for transportation; however, dog sled races (d) <u>are</u> still a popular sport during the cold winters.

26. The men or women who (a) <u>race</u> dog sleds are "mushers." (b) <u>For</u> many years before the race, they (c) <u>have</u> (d) <u>been trained</u> their dogs to pull the sled and to work together as a team.

27. One of the most famous dog sled races is the Iditarod Trail. It (a) <u>covers</u> more than 1,000 miles of Alaskan wilderness. Even today, this race (b) <u>had</u> (c) <u>challenged</u> mushers and their dogs (d) <u>for</u> many years.

28. (a) <u>You have</u> (b) <u>ever</u> (c) <u>slept</u> outside in the middle of winter? Mushers and their dogs (d) <u>sleep</u> in snow camps during the race.

29. My brother (a) <u>have</u> (b) <u>watched</u> the start of the Iditarod Trail race several times, but he (c) <u>hasn't ever</u> (d) <u>watched</u> the finish.

30. (a) <u>Last week</u>, I (b) <u>saw</u> this great race for the first time. I (c) <u>watched</u> the beginning of the race in Anchorage, and then I (d) <u>have flown</u> to Nome, Alaska, to see the finish.

31. It (a) <u>was</u> (b) <u>exciting</u> to watch the dogs and the mushers cross the finish line. All of the people (c) <u>have been</u> (d) <u>shouting</u> to encourage the mushers and his dogs.

32. I (a) <u>haven't known</u> that Alaskan winters were so exciting. You (b) <u>have</u> (c) <u>really</u> (d) <u>had</u> a great vacation.

MAKING OFFERS WITH *WOULD YOU LIKE*

 EXERCISE 1   *(Focus 1 and 2, page 240)*

Pierre Eclair has just become the new assistant manager of the Gourmet Diner. He is trying to make the atmosphere a little more elegant and sophisticated, so he is listening to how the waitresses talk to their customers. Read the dialogue between Wanda the waitress and her customers, Phil and Emily. Then rewrite the dialogue using polite forms. The first one has been done for you as an example.

Wanda: Good morning. Where do you want to sit? <u>Good morning. Where would you like to sit?</u>

           Do you want a table by the window? _____

Phil: Yes, that would be fine.

Wanda: Want some coffee? _____

Phil: Yes, please, two cups of coffee.

Wanda: Sugar or cream in your coffee? _____

Phil: Sugar for me, please . . .

Wanda: Here's your coffee.

           Do you want to order now? _____

Phil: Yes, I guess we do.

Wanda: What do you want? _____

Emily: I'll have eggs and French toast.

Wanda: How do you want your eggs? _____

Emily: Fried, but not too well done.

Wanda: Do you want me to tell the cook to make them over easy? _____

_____

Emily: Yes, please.

Wanda: And you, sir? Do you want eggs, too? _____

_____

Phil: Yes, I'll have the cheese omelet with hash browns.

Wanda: Need anything else? _____

Phil: Yes, some orange juice.

Wanda: Great. I'll be back with your breakfast in a moment.

Read the description of the conversations between Marc Antony and Cleopatra on their first date, and then on another date a year later. Write the dialogues using *would you like* or *do you want*, as appropriate. Marc Antony's first line has been written for you as an example.

First Date

MARC ANTONY	**CLEOPATRA**
1. asks Cleopatra for a date	2. accepts the offer
3. asks Cleopatra what kind of restaurant she wants to go to	4. says she prefers French or Italian
5. asks what movie Cleopatra wants to see	6. tells him which movie she wants to see

Marc Antony:

   1. <u>Would you like to go out with me this weekend?</u>

Cleopatra:

   2. _____

Marc Antony:

   3. _____

Cleopatra:

   4. _____

Marc Antony:

   5. _____

Cleopatra:

   6. _____

One Year Later

MARC ANTONY	CLEOPATRA
7. asks Cleopatra if she wants to stay home and watch the football game	8. says she prefers to go country-western dancing
9. asks if she wants to order out for pizza	10. says she prefers Chinese food
11. asks her if she wants to go bowling and eat at the bowling alley instead	12. she accepts

Marc Antony:

7. _____

Cleopatra:

8. _____

Marc Antony:

9. _____

Cleopatra:

10. _____

Marc Antony:

11. _____

Cleopatra:

12. _____

Write a dialogue for each of the following situations. Be sure to consider the politeness level of the situation. If the offer is refused, have the person give a reason for the refusal. The first dialogue has been started for you. Explain why you choose to make the polite request formal or informal.

1. A flight attendant on an airplane offers a passenger lunch. The passenger isn't hungry but would like something to drink.

   Flight Attendant: <u>Would you like some lunch?</u>

   Passenger: _____

   _____

   Explanation: <u>The flight attendant would use a formal request because her job is to serve the</u> <u>passenger and she does not know him personally.</u>

2. A father offers to help his son with his homework. The son really needs help.

   _____

   _____

   Explanation: _____

   _____

3. One of your classmates looks confused by directions on an assignment. You offer to help her. She accepts.

   _____

   _____

   Explanation: _____

   _____

4. A woman with two small children and many packages is trying to get on a bus. You offer to help her. She accepts.

   _____

   _____

   Explanation: _____

   _____

5. An elderly man is standing at the corner. He looks lost. Another man offers to help him. The elderly man explains that he is waiting for his son.

   _____

   _____

   Explanation: _____

   _____

6. Your friend visits you on a hot summer day. You offer her a glass of lemonade. She gladly accepts.

_____

_____

Explanation: _____

_____

7. Your father's friend is in your city for a couple of days. You offer to show him the sights. He is not able to accept your offer because he has to attend a business meeting.

_____

_____

Explanation: _____

_____

8. Deb's husband has a headache. She offers to get him some aspirin. He accepts.

_____

_____

Explanation: _____

_____

■ EXERCISE 4 _(Focus 3, page 242)_

Below are situations in which you might make a request. Work with a partner and write dialogues for each situation. Act out some of the dialogues for your classmates.

Example: On a subway train
Those packages look heavy. Would you like me to hold them for you?
Yes, thanks. It's hard to stand up on the train and hold them.

1. Someone is sick _____

_____

2. It's the first day at a new school _____

_____

3. At a restaurant _____

_____

4. In a department store _____

_____

5. At a picnic _____

_____

6. At a travel agency _____

_____

REQUESTS AND PERMISSION
Can, Could, Will, Would, and May

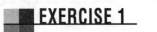 **EXERCISE 1** *(Focus 1, page 250)*

Below are some situations in which requests are commonly made. For each situation, write a request using *can*, *could*, *will*, *would*, or *may*, as appropriate.

Example: You're driving to a party with a friend. You're not sure exactly where the party is. You say to your friend:
Could you look up the directions on the computer, please? I'm not exactly sure how to get to the party.

1. You aren't sure which bus goes to the beach. You see a man waiting at the bus stop. You say:

   _____

   _____

2. After you find out which bus to take, you want to know how often it stops here. You ask the man:

   _____

   _____

3. When you come home from shopping, your arms are full of packages. You see your neighbor near the front door of your apartment building. You say:

   _____

   _____

4. You have to be at work a half hour early tomorrow. Your husband/wife always gets up before you and wakes you up. You say to him or her:

   _____

   _____

5. You are looking for your seats in a theater. You see an usher and ask:

   _____

   _____

6. You forgot to buy milk when you went to the grocery store. You ask your roommate to stop and get some:

   _____

   _____

7. You're giving a dinner party. Suddenly you realize you are out of eggs, which you need for your dessert. You phone your neighbor and ask:

_____

_____

8. You're trying to find the immigration building. You know it's nearby. You approach a woman and say:

_____

_____

9. You see the kind of cake mix you want to buy on the top shelf, but you can't reach it. You ask another customer to reach the box for you:

_____

_____

EXERCISE 2   (Focus 2, page 251)

Imagine someone made the polite requests below, but you must refuse the request. Explain why you are refusing and use a softening phrase.

Example: Can you lend me your book?
               I'd like to, but I can't. I left my book at home today.

1. Could you help me with this math problem? _____

_____

2. May I borrow a dollar? _____

_____

3. Would you please help me get my ball down from the tree? _____

_____

4. My car has a flat tire. Will you please help me change it? _____

_____

5. May I please have some more orange juice? _____

_____

6. Mom, will you please help me practice my lines for the play? _____

_____

7. My car is broken. Can you please give me a ride tomorrow? _____

_____

8. If you are going out, would you please return my library books? _____

_____

9. Please make copies of these documents. _____

_____

Hana is a flight attendant. Passengers often make requests of her. Following are some requests the passengers have made. Write Hana's response to each request, varying the responses.

Example: Could you help me put this bag in the bin? <u>Sure, I would be happy to.</u>

1. Could you get me a pillow? _____

_____

2. Would you bring me some more sugar for my coffee, please? _____

_____

3. Can you show me where the bathrooms are? _____

_____

4. May I have another drink? _____

_____

5. Will you take away my food tray? _____

_____

6. Can you tell me where to catch my connecting flight? _____

_____

7. Could you help me find the list of movies on this flight? _____

_____

8. Would you get me a magazine? _____

_____

9. Will you turn down the air conditioning? I can't reach it. _____

_____

10. May I have some earphones? _____

_____

Below are some situations where a person might ask for permission. For each situation, write a permission question. Use *would*, *may*, or *do (would) you mind if*, as appropriate.

Example: You get a chance to meet your favorite singer. Ask for permission to take his or her picture.
Would you mind if I took your picture?

1. A young girl wants to spend the night at a friend's house this weekend. She asks her mother for permission.

   _____

   _____

2. Gus is at a formal dinner party and needs to leave the table for a minute. He asks the hostess for permission.

   _____

   _____

3. You are at a friend's house. You would like to smoke, but you're not sure whether it is allowed. Ask permission to smoke.

   _____

   _____

4. You have a friend coming from Japan to visit. You'd like your friend to see what an American school is like. Ask permission from your teacher to bring your friend to class.

   _____

   _____

5. Your community organization is having a special summer program for children. Ask the owner of the drugstore for permission to put one of your posters about the program in his stone window.

   _____

   _____

6. You have a doctor's appointment at 4:00. Ask your boss for permission to leave work early.

   _____

   _____

7. Your classroom is getting a little hot and stuffy. Ask your teacher for permission to open the window.

   _____

   _____

8. You find an interesting magazine at the library. You're not sure whether you can check out magazines. Ask the librarian for permission to check the magazine out.

   _____

   _____

9. You park your car by an office building. You are not sure whether parking is permitted. Ask the security guard for permission to park there.

_____

_____

10. You need to visit your counselor. Ask permission from your teacher.

_____

_____

■ EXERCISE 5   (Focus 5, page 256)

Below are the reactions of each person who was asked permission for something in Exercise 4. Use the information from Exercise 4 and the information below to write appropriate responses. If permission is refused, use a softening phrase and tell why the request is refused.

Example: The singer says "yes."
          Sure, you can take my picture.

1. The girl's mother says no.

_____

2. The hostess says yes.

_____

3. Your friend doesn't allow smoking in the house.

_____

4. Your teacher says yes.

_____

5. The owner gives permission.

_____

6. Your boss doesn't give permission.

_____

7. Your teacher says yes.

_____

8. The librarian says no.

_____

9. The security guard says no.

_____

10. Your teacher says yes.

_____

USED TO WITH *STILL* AND *ANYMORE*

EXERCISE 1   *(Focus 1, page 264)*

Circle T if the statement is true, and F if the statement is false.

1.	People used to use candles and gas lamps because they didn't have electricity.	T	F
2.	Before electricity, people used to put a big block of ice in the *icebox*; today we use a refrigerator.	T	F
3.	Before electricity, people used to use batteries for power.	T	F
4.	Before the invention of the car, people used to ride the bus.	T	F
5.	People used to walk much more than they do now.	T	F
6.	There didn't use to be as much violent crime as there is now.	T	F
7.	People used to know much more about nutrition than they do now.	T	F
8.	Big families used to be much more common than they are now.	T	F
9.	People used to live longer than they do now.	T	F
10.	There didn't use to be a big drug problem.	T	F

EXERCISE 2   *(Focus 2, page 265)*

Using the words below, ask and answer questions with the correct form of *used to*.

Example: You / have long hair?
          Did you use to have long hair?
          Yes, I used to have very long hair.

1. Where / you / live? _____

   _____

2. When you were a little boy/girl, what / you / play? _____

   _____

3. When you were in elementary school, what / you / do after school? _____

   _____

4. When you were very young, / your parents / read to you? _____

_____

5. What bad habit / you / have? _____

_____

6. What / you / look like? _____

_____

7. Who / be your best friend? _____

_____

8. / you / live in the city or the country? _____

_____

9. Where / you / go on vacation? _____

_____

10. / you / wear glasses? _____

_____

■ EXERCISE 3   *(Focus 3, page 265)*

Fill in the blank with the correct form of *used to* or *anymore*.

My grandmother complains about how things have changed, and she says that life (1) _____
be better.

Families aren't families the way they (2) _____ be. Everyone's divorced. If a husband and
wife are having problems with their marriage, they don't stay together (3) _____. And mothers
(4) _____ stay home and take care of their children, but not (5) _____. Everyone's
working. No one has time for children (6) _____.

And the cars! No one walks (7) _____; everybody drives. We (8) _____ walk
five miles to school every day, even in the winter. And in school, the children don't have to think
(9) _____. In math class, for example, we (10) _____ add, subtract, multiply,
and divide, using our heads. Kids don't use their heads (11) _____; they use calculators.

Computers have taken control over our lives. In my day, we didn't have computers. We didn't even
have electricity. My mother (12) _____ spend all day cooking in the kitchen. Nobody eats
home-cooked food (13) _____. Food (14) _____ taste better. It's all chemicals
and preservatives now.

And people don't talk to each other (15) _____. They're too busy to talk, too busy to eat,
too busy to think . . .

Life (16) _____ be simple, but it isn't (17) _____.

EXERCISE 4 (Focus 4, page 266)

Circle T if the statement is true, and F if it is false. Correct the false statements to make them true. Use *still*, *used to*, or *anymore*.

1. There used to be a country called the Soviet Union, but there isn't anymore. T F
2. There used to be a city called Moscow in Russia, but there isn't anymore. T F
3. There's still a country called Algeria in North Africa. T F
4. The Golden Gate Bridge used to be in Chicago. T F
5. They still haven't found the lost city of Atlantis. T F
6. Antony and Cleopatra still float down the Nile River. T F
7. They used to speak Icelandic in Ireland, but they don't anymore. T F
8. There used to be a wall separating East and West Germany, but there isn't anymore. T F
9. Alaska used to belong to Russia, but it doesn't anymore. T F
10. The Taj Mahal used to be in Egypt, but it isn't anymore. T F
11. Uzbekistan used to be part of the Soviet Union. T F
12. Tanzania is still in Antarctica. T F

EXERCISE 5 (Focus 4, page 266)

Holly and Greta have been friends since high school. Greta just went to their 20-year high-school reunion, but Holly couldn't go. In the following dialogue, they are talking about their former classmates. Look at the picture and complete the dialogue, using the correct form of the verb in parentheses and *still* or *anymore*. Be careful—many of the sentences are negative.

20 years ago

Jim

today

Holly: Did you see Jim Jensen? He used to be so wild!

Greta: (1) Yes, but he _____. (be) He looks very conservative now.

Holly: Was he thin in high school? I don't remember.

Greta: (2) Yes, and he _____. (be)

Holly: (3) _____? (he, wear glasses)

Greta: Yes, he does.

Holly: (4) _____? (he, play the guitar)

Greta: Yes, he does, but now he plays classical guitar. He (5) _____. (play rock and roll)

Holly: Didn't he use to have long hair?

Greta: (6) Yes, he did, but he _____. Now he's bald. I also saw Jan Bissing at the reunion. Remember her? She used to be the most popular girl in school.

Jan

20 years ago   today

Holly: (7) What does she look like now? _____ the same? (she, look)

Greta: (8) Yes, except for her hair. She _____ (have long, brown hair). Now it's short and blonde. But she (9) _____! (be, cute) She (10) _____ those big blue eyes and those thick eyelashes. (have)

Holly: There was something different about her . . . didn't she always use to wear a hat?

Greta: (11) Yes, and she _____.

Holly: Didn't she and George Weissler use to be a couple?

Greta: (12) They _____(be)! They've been married for 18 years.

Look at the information in the chart, and answer the questions, using *still*, *anymore*, or an adverb of frequency. Be careful with verb tenses.

Carol used to be single. Last year she married George. George is divorced and has two children. The chart shows how Carol's life has changed.

	BEFORE	NOW
always	go dancing on weekends	stay home on weekends
often / usually	go out to eat travel go to the gym and work out	cook dinner clean the house do the laundry every day
sometimes	read novels go to the beach	help kids with homework go to the beach go to baseball games
seldom / hardly ever	cook clean	read novels go out to eat
never	stay home on weekends go to baseball games have children	go dancing travel

1. Before she got married, how often did Carol use to go dancing?

_____

2. Did Carol use to have children?

_____

3. Does Carol ever help the kids with their homework?

_____

4. When she was single, what did Carol use to do on her vacation?

_____

5. Did Carol ever use to cook and clean?

_____

6. Does Carol ever cook and clean now?

_____

7. Does Carol still go dancing?

_____

8. Does she still go to the beach?

_____

9. Does she go out to eat every night?

_____

10. How often does she do the laundry?

_____

Choose the *one* word or phrase (*a, b, c,* or *d*) that best completes each sentence. Then circle the letter.

1. Would you carry this notebook for me? Sure, I _____.

   a. can

   b. could

   c. will

   d. may

2. _____ lend me your calculator? I left mine at home.

   a. May you

   b. Would you

   c. Would you like

   d. Might you

3. _____ but the batteries in my calculator have gone dead. It doesn't work.

   a. Yes,

   b. Sure,

   c. No problem,

   d. I'd like to,

4. I used to do my assignments by myself, _____.

   a. but I don't do that anymore

   b. but I still do that

   c. and I still do that

   d. and I don't do that anymore

5. I _____ frustrated when I wasn't sure of the correct answer.

   a. may be

   b. used to

   c. used to be

   d. use to be

6. _____ to compare your answers with mine? That way we could both check our homework.

   a. Do you like

   b. Would you like

   c. May you like

   d. Could you like

7. That's a great idea. _____ you move your desk over here so we can compare answers?

   a. May

   b. Do

   c. Would

   d. Did

8. _____ you mind if I skip the movies tonight? I have a headache.

   a. Could

   b. Will

   c. Would

   d. May

9. The dog looks thirsty. _____ some water?

   a. Would you mind   c. Want

   b. Would they like   d. Does it want

10. _____ work downtown?

   a. Did you used to   c. Do you used to

   b. Did you use to   d. Do you use to

EDITING PRACTICE

Questions 11–20: Identify the *one* underlined word or phrase that must be changed for the sentence to be grammatically correct.

11. (a) <u>Would you</u> help me, (b) <u>please</u>? I'm trying to get to South Mall. (c) <u>You can</u> tell me what bus I (d) <u>should</u> take?

12. This (a) <u>isn't</u> the right bus stop. (b) <u>Do</u> (c) <u>you like</u> me (d) <u>to show</u> you the way to the bus stop?

13. Yes, (a) <u>please</u>, (b) <u>could you</u> show me the way? I (c) <u>use to</u> know where all the buses stopped, but I (d) <u>haven't taken</u> a bus in a long time.

14. (a) <u>No problem</u>. The buses to downtown don't stop here (b) <u>still</u>. You (c) <u>could</u> take either the 3 or the 16 bus. The bus stop is there, (d) <u>across</u> the street.

15. (a) <u>May you</u> help me? (b) <u>Sure</u>. What do you need? (c) <u>Could you</u> (d) <u>please</u> reach that jar on the top shelf? It's too high for me.

16. (a) <u>May</u> I borrow your pencil? Yes, (b) <u>you would</u>. (c) <u>Thanks</u>. (d) <u>No problem</u>.

17. (a) <u>Want</u> some help with that? (b) <u>No thanks</u>. I'm (c) <u>used to</u> (d) <u>do</u> it by myself.

18. I (a) <u>used to</u> (b) <u>go</u> the whole night without sleep, (c) <u>but</u> (d) <u>anymore</u> I can't do that.

19. (a) <u>Would you like</u> (b) <u>to be meeting</u> my uncle? He's very funny. He (c) <u>used to tell</u> us jokes all night, and I think he (d) <u>still tells</u> great jokes.

20. (a) <u>Should you</u> help me find my car keys? I (b) <u>can't</u> find them anywhere. I'm sorry (c) <u>I can't</u> help you now. I'm late for work, but (d) <u>I could</u> ask Celia to help you find them.

PAST PERFECT
Before and *After*

EXERCISE 1   *(Focus 1, page 274)*

Read about Jerry, and then fill in the time line with information from Jerry's life. Include only the underlined verbs. The first one has been done for you.

Jerry Zimmerman used to be a typical young man. Then five years ago, a car accident changed his life forever. The accident paralyzed him, and now he'<u>s</u> in a wheelchair.

After the accident, Jerry <u>was</u> in the hospital for a long time. He <u>had</u> a lot of operations. He <u>had never been</u> in the hospital before, and he <u>had never seen</u> so many doctors: surgeons, anesthesiologists, neurologists, . . . He <u>had never felt</u> so much pain; he was sure the physical therapists were experts in torture. He <u>had to learn</u> to get around in a wheelchair, too.

Before the accident, Jerry <u>had played</u> tennis and he <u>had sailed</u>. Now <u>he's learning to play</u> table tennis, and he still <u>sails</u> his boat on the lake near his house. He also <u>competes</u> in races in his wheelchair. He <u>had always had</u> a dog, but after the accident, he <u>needed</u> a specially trained dog to help him around the house. Last year he <u>got</u> Connie, a Black Labrador.

As for his love life, Jerry <u>had been</u> engaged to a girl named Debbie. He's still going to be married, but now he'<u>s</u> engaged to Patty—his physical therapist.

BEFORE ACCIDENT	AFTER ACCIDENT	NOW
1. Jerry had never been in the hospital.	1. Jerry was in the hospital.	1. He's in a wheelchair.
2.	2.	2.
3.	3.	3.
4.	4.	4.
5.	5.	5.
6.		

EXERCISE 2   (Focus 2, page 274)

A reporter is interviewing Jerry (Exercise 1) for a feature story about people with disabilities. The reporter wants to know about Jerry's life before he was paralyzed. Using the words given below, write the reporter's questions and Jerry's answers. Use the past perfect.

Example: your life / pretty normal?
Had your life been pretty normal? Yes, it had.

1. How many times / you / be in the hospital / before the accident?

   _____

   _____

2. What sports / you / play / before the accident?

   _____

   _____

3. you / run in races?

   _____

   _____

4. Before Connie, / you / have a dog?

   _____

   _____

Combine the following pairs of statements to make one sentence, using the word in parentheses to connect them. Change one of the verbs into the past perfect. The first one has been done for you.

1. He had a fight with his wife.

   Allen slept badly last night. (because)

   <u>Allen slept badly last night because he had had a fight with his wife.</u>

   _____

2. He slept late this morning.

   Nobody set the alarm. (because)

   _____

   _____

3. Nobody did the laundry.

   Allen didn't have any clean underwear. (so)

   _____

   _____

4. Nobody went grocery shopping.

   There wasn't any coffee. (because)

   _____

   _____

5. Allen forgot to go to the gas station.

   There wasn't any gas in the car. (because)

   _____

   _____

6. He was very worried.

   His boss told him not to be late anymore. (so)

   _____

   _____

7. He looked in the mirror and saw that he didn't comb his hair.

   He was driving. (while)

   _____

   _____

8. He realized that he didn't cash his paycheck.

   He got to the gas station. (when)

   _____

   _____

9. Allen found that he left his wallet at the gas station.

He got to work. (as soon as)

_____

_____

10. He noticed there were no cars in the parking lot.

He realized that he forgot it was Saturday. (when)

_____

_____

EXERCISE 4 *(Focus 3, page 277)*

In each of the following sentences, write 1 over the action that occurred first, and 2 over the action that was second. If there are three verbs, write 3 over the third action. Then check (✓) the sentences where it is necessary to use the past perfect to indicate the order of events. The first one has been done for you.

1. _____ Last night Mr. Wilson walked the dog and then let the cat out.
   (1 over "walked the dog", 2 over "let the cat out")

2. _____ He locked the doors, turned off the lights, and went upstairs.

3. _____ When he got upstairs, he realized that he had forgotten to take out the garbage.

4. _____ He went back downstairs and took out the garbage.

5. _____ When he went upstairs to brush his teeth, he heard a noise.

6. _____ By the time Mr. Wilson got to the door, the noise had stopped.

7. _____ He went back upstairs and heard the noise again. It sounded like someone crying.

8. _____ He went back downstairs, and again, before he reached the door, the noise had stopped.

9. _____ By that time, Mr. Wilson had gone up and down the stairs so many times that he was dizzy. He went to bed.

10. _____ The next morning when Mr. Wilson went outside to get the newspaper, he saw what had caused the noise the night before.

11. _____ He was surprised to see that the cat had had kittens.

EXERCISE 5 *(Focus 3, page 277)*

Use *before, after, by the time,* or *by* to answer the following questions about Mr. Wilson (Exercise 4) with complete sentences. The first one has been done for you.

1. Did Mr. Wilson walk the dog last night?
   <u>Yes, he walked the dog before he let the cat out.</u>

2. What had Mr. Wilson done by the time he locked the doors and turned off the lights?

_____

3. What was he doing when he first heard the noise?

_____

4. What did Mr. Wilson do when he heard the noise?

_____

5. Why did he first go back downstairs?

_____

6. Did Mr. Wilson hear the noise before or after he went upstairs?

_____

7. Why did he feel dizzy?

_____

8. By the time he went to bed, how many times had Mr. Wilson walked up the stairs?

_____

9. What had caused the noise?

_____

■ EXERCISE 6   (Focus 4, page 278)

For each space below, write the correct tense (simple past, past perfect, present perfect, simple present, or present progressive) of the verb in parentheses. If there's another word in parentheses, include it in your answer. The first one has been done for you.

Last winter Yarima Good (1) _____took_____ (take) a trip into the past. She (2) _____
(go) to visit her people, the Yanomama, in South America, one of the most primitive cultures on Earth.

   Yarima (3) _____ (go) from the Stone Age to the twentieth century six years ago.
Before then, she (4) _____ (wear, never) clothes or (5) _____ (be) in shoes.
Since then, she (6) _____ (learn) to make light with a little plastic thing on the wall. She
(7) _____ (learn, also) not to be afraid of mirrors or toilets or cars.

   Anthropologist Kenneth Good first (8) _____ (visit) South America in 1975. He
(9) _____ (be) the first *nabuh*, or outsider, Yarima (10) _____ (see, ever).
She (11) _____ (be) a child then; she (12) _____ (be) 14 years old. Ken
(13) _____ (stay) with the Yanomama people for 12 years. As a child, Yarima
(14) _____ (fish) with him in the river; then she (15) _____ (grow) up. They
(16) _____ (fall) in love and (17) _____ (get) married.

   Now Yarima (18) _____ (be) the stranger, the *nabuh*, living in a place where everything
(19) _____ (be) different. She (20) _____ (have) three children, and because
of them, she (21) _____ (have) to live in this new world outside of New York City. For the
Yanomama, the only counting system is *one, two,* and *many,* so Yarima's tutor (22) _____
(teach) her to count. She (23) _____, (learn) but it (24) _____ (be, not) easy.

   Ken Good (25) _____ (write) a book about his Amazon adventure, *Into the Heart.*

(Based on "Stone Age to Suburbs," by Nancy Shulins, Associated Press, *Miami Herald,* January 3, 1992.)

ARTICLES
The, A/An, Some and *Ø*

 EXERCISE 1   *(Focus 1, page 286)*

Olena is a new student at Georgia Perimeter College. She needs to buy her books and supplies for the next semester. The helpful bookstore assistant is helping her get everything she needs. Fill in the blanks with *the, a, an, Ø (no article),* or *some*. The first one has been done for you as an example.

CLASS	TEXTBOOK	OTHER SUPPLIES
Biology	*Human Biology,* 2nd Edition	Anatomy Chart; Anatomy Flashcards
French	*Voilà!,* 5th Edition	Notebook, 2 audio CDs
English Composition	*Inventing Arguments*	Notebook (8 1/2 x 11), computer software
Math	*Essential Calculus*	TI-89 plus calculator

Assistant: Are you taking ____*a*____ biology course?

   Olena: Yes, I'm taking (1) _____ Human Biology. I need (2) _____ 2nd Edition of *Human Biology*.

Assistant: Do you need anything else for that class?

   Olena: Sure. I need (3) _____ Anatomy Chart and (4) _____ Anatomy Flash Cards.

Assistant: What foreign language course are you taking?

   Olena: I'm taking (5) _____ French course. I'll need to buy (6) _____ 5th edition of *Voilà!* I also need (7) _____ notebook and (8) _____ 2 audio CDs.

Assistant: Do you need any other (9) _____ notebooks?

   Olena: Yes, I need (10) _____ 8 1/2 x 11 notebook for English Composition.

Assistant: So, you need (11) _____ two notebooks.

Using the information on the chart, continue the conversation between Olena and the Assistant. Be sure to use *the, a, an, Ø (no article),* or *some* correctly.

Assistant: _____

   Olena: _____

Assistant: _____

   Olena: _____

Read the following story. Is the article usage correct for each underlined noun phrase? If the article usage is not correct, write the correct usage above the underlined words.

A FRACTURED FAIRY TALE

One morning Papa Bear, Mama Bear, and Baby Bear couldn't eat their porridge because it was too hot. So <u>the</u> three bears went for (1) <u>a walk</u> while their porridge cooled. While they were gone, Goldilocks came in. She saw (2) <u>a porridge</u> cooling. First, she tried Papa's bowl, but (3) <u>the porridge</u> was too hot. Next, she tried Mama's bowl, but (4) <u>a porridge</u> was too cold. Finally, she tried Baby Bear's porridge, and it was just right, so she ate it all up.

After that, Goldilocks was tired, so she looked for (5) <u>the place</u> to rest. She found (6) <u>the bedrooms</u>. She tried Papa's room, but (7) <u>a bed</u> was too hard. Then she tried Mama's bed, but it was too soft. Finally, she tried Baby's bed, and it was just right. She felt so comfortable that she fell asleep.

When (8) <u>the bears</u> came home, they found (9) <u>the big surprise</u>. Papa Bear looked at (10) <u>a spoon</u> in his bowl and said, "Someone has been eating my porridge."

Mama Bear looked at (11) <u>a spoon</u> in her bowl and said, "Someone has been eating (12) <u>the porridge</u>, all right."

When he looked at his bowl, Baby Bear began to cry; (13) <u>a bowl</u> was empty. When Mama went to her bedroom, she found (14) <u>the blankets</u> in a mess.

"Look, Papa, (15) <u>the beds</u> are a mess."

"You're right," Papa Bear agreed. "Someone has been sleeping in my bed, too."

"Here she is!" shouted Baby Bear.

At the sound of Baby Bear's voice. Goldilocks jumped up and ran out.

However, (16) <u>the police officer</u> was near (17) <u>a bear's house</u>. Goldilocks was arrested. She was charged with unlawful entry, stealing porridge, and bad manners. (18) <u>the judge</u> sent her to Miss Manners' School of Etiquette for three months.

Complete this story by filling the blanks with either *a, an, some*, or Ø *(no article)*. The first one has been done for you.

HIGH-WIRE ORANGUTANS

Have you ever seen ____*an*____ orangutan swinging above you? At the National Zoo in Washington, D.C., the orangutans go from their home in the great ape house to (1) _____ special orangutan school called the Think Tank. Zookeepers don't take the orangutan to the Think Tank. The orangutans get there on their own. (2) _____ high tower stands in the orangutan yard at the great ape house. (3) _____ cables connect the tower to five other towers. If he wants, (4) _____ adventurous orangutan can travel across the cables. On each tower there is (5) _____ platform where the orangutans can take (6) _____ rest. (7) _____ electrified set of wires beneath the platform keeps the orangutans from going below. Swinging along the cables, (8) _____ orangutans can see (9) _____ ornamental duck pond and (10) _____ people walking below. This is (11) _____ unique experience for the orangutans. No other zoo has such (12) _____ facility.

(13) _____ modern zoos are different from the zoos of just twenty years ago. In the past, (14) _____ animals were shut in small cages. Today zoos are encouraging animals to use their natural talents. Now (15) _____ animals have more (16) _____ freedom.

■ EXERCISE 4   *(Focus 4, page 290)*

Fill in the blanks with *some* or Ø *(no article).* If both are appropriate, write both answers. The first one has been done for you as an example.

Beth: Would you like to listen to <u>some, Ø</u> music or watch (1) _____ movies?

 Joe: What kind of music do you have?

Beth: I have (2) _____ jazz and (3) _____ Brazilian music.

 Joe: Brazilian Music?

Beth: (4) _____ Samba and (5) _____ Bossa Nova are types of Brazilian music.

 Joe: I think I'd rather watch a movie.

Beth: Great, I'll get (6) _____ snacks and (7) _____ drinks.

 Joe: Great. I'll get the DVD player set up. What kind of snacks do you have?

Beth: I can make (8) _____ popcorn and I have (9) _____ corn chips.

 Joe: What kind of (10) _____ corn chips do you have?

■ EXERCISE 5   *(Focus 5, page 291)*

Fill in the blanks in the story with *a, some, the,* or Ø *(no article.)*

Let me give you some advice on how to choose (1) _____ college. First, you want to decide what type of (2) _____ college is best for you. It's best to do (3) _____ research about (4) _____ colleges on (5) _____ Internet. First, it's important to know if you have (6) _____ money you need to pay for (7) _____ college you want to attend. You should also make sure you can study (8) _____ major that you choose. If you want to study (9) _____ Biology, you don't want to end up at (10) _____ college that doesn't have (11) _____ biology lab. Finally you should, take (12) _____ time to visit (13) _____ college before you go there.

Complete the following story by filling each blank with *the* or Ø *(no article)*. The first one has been done for you.

Newfoundland is one province of Canada that attracts ____Ø____ tourists of all ages. Much of (1) _____ province is on Newfoundland Island and is separated from Canada's mainland. (2) _____ ferries and (3) _____ airplanes bring (4) _____ passengers from all over (5) _____ world. (6) _____ rugged coast of this island is full of (7) _____ natural beauty. (8) _____ tourists marvel at (9) _____ inlets in Gros Morne National Park. (10) _____ nature is everywhere on Newfoundland Island. (11) _____ people watch for (12) _____ birds such as (13) _____ eagles, (14) _____ cormorants, and (15) _____ gillemots, or they look for (16) _____ pilot whales in (17) _____ water. Yes, (18) _____ life is beautiful on Newfoundland Island.

For each group of words write a sentence that reflects the meaning of the words.

Example: The city (locally) *The city looks beautiful at night. (The speaker is looking at a specific city.)*
The city (regionally) *I'm driving to the city. (There is only one city in the region.)*
The city (universally) *Sociologists study the city. (Everyone has an idea of what a city is.)*

1. The computer (locally) _____

_____

2. The computer (universally) _____

_____

3. The mountains (locally) _____

_____

4. The mountains (regionally) _____

_____

5. The fish (locally) _____

_____

6. The fish (universally) _____

_____

7. The movies (locally) _____

_____

8. The movies (universally) _____

_____

Complete this weather report by filling each blank with *a, an,* or *the.* The first one has been done for you.

Now it's time for (1) ___the___ nightly weather report. (2) _____ weather looks pretty messy out there.
This was (3) _____ rainiest day ever for (4) _____ first day of summer. There were showers and
thunderstorms from (5) _____ mountains to (6) _____ coast.

   (7) _____ strong thunderstorm struck (8) _____ west side of the city tonight. (9) _____
old oak tree was hit by lightning and burned. Fortunately, no one was hurt.

   It wasn't (10) _____ good day for getting (11) _____ look at (12) _____ sun, but
(13) _____ rain was needed. This has been (14) _____ driest spring on record. (15) _____
plants and trees really needed (16) _____ rain.

   (17) _____ high temperature was 72°. (18) _____ three-day forecast calls for more rain.
But don't worry, things will clear up. We will have (19) _____ excellent weekend.

ARTICLES WITH NAMES OF PLACES

Read the description of Canada on the next page. Circle the geographical names that do not take articles and underline the geographical names that take articles. The first sentence has been done for you.

CANADA

(Canada) is the northernmost country in North America. Canada is bordered by the United States on the south, the Arctic Ocean on the north, the Atlantic Ocean on the east, and the Pacific Ocean and Alaska on the west. Canada is divided into ten provinces and three territories. Quebec is the largest province, and Prince Edward Island is the smallest province. The two largest cities in Canada are Montreal and Toronto. The two highest mountains in Canada are Mount Logan and Mount St. Elias, which are located in the Rocky Mountains. The Great Lakes are part of Canada's southern border. Lake Huron is the largest lake in Canada. The most important rivers in Canada are the St. Lawrence River and the Mackenzie River.

EXERCISE 2   *(Focus 1, page 304)*

Write a paragraph about the geography of your native country. If necessary, use the Internet for help with specific facts. Include information about rivers, lakes, deserts, mountains, cities, states or provinces, and neighboring countries.

EXERCISE 3   *(Focus 1, page 304)*

Test your knowledge of world geography. Name a geographical location for each category that begins with the letter at the top of the column. Be sure to include articles for the places that require them.

	M	G	S
Rivers			
Deserts			
Cities			
Lakes			

	H	A	R
Islands and island chains			
Mountain chains or peaks			
Streets in your city			

	P	M	N
States or provinces			
Planets			
Oceans or seas			

Complete the following story by writing *the* or Ø in each blank, as appropriate. The first one has been done for you.

In 2005, Hurricanes Katrina and Rita destroyed more property than any other natural disaster in the United States. Not only did it destroy homes and businesses; many public institutions were also damaged.

All of the colleges and universities in the area were damaged. (1) __The__ University of New Orleans and (2) _____ Tulane University closed for the fall semester. (3) _____ Dillard University and (4) _____ University of Louisiana's Xavier campus were also heavily damaged.

Historical buildings, like (5) _____ Tullis Toledano Manor in Biloxi, Mississippi, was completely destroyed. Historical buildings like (6) _____ 1850 House and (7) _____ Edgar Degas House also suffered damage.

Also, some of the hospitals—for example (8) _____ Charity Hospital and (9) _____ Tulane Medical Center—were unable to evacuate some of their patients.

New Orleans is famous for its tourist attractions. (10) _____ French Quarter was spared the most severe damage. (11) _____ Audubon Zoo lost many trees, but most of the animals were safe. The most badly damaged attraction was (12) _____ Aquarium of the Americas. Almost all of the fish and marine life were destroyed.

Choose the word, group of words, or phrase (*a, b, c,* or *d*) that best completes each sentence. Then circle the letter.

1. I like fruit. I had _____ banana and _____ apple for lunch.

   a. the . . . the

   b. a . . . a

   c. an . . . a

   d. a . . . an

2. _____ your assignment before class started?

   a. Had you finished

   b. When you finished

   c. Do you finish

   d. You had finishing

3. _____ famous volcano in North America is Mt. St. Helens, which erupted in 1980.

   a. One of most

   b. One of the most

   c. The most

   d. The more

4. The tallest building in Canada is _____, which is located in _____.

   a. CN Tower . . . Toronto

   b. the CN Tower . . . Toronto

   c. the CN Tower . . . the Toronto

   d. CN Tower . . . the Toronto

5. We _____ in the ocean before we went to California.

   a. had never swam

   b. have never swum

   c. hadn't swam

   d. had never swum

6. I like the theater. I would like to see _____ more plays.

   a. the

   b. a

   c. an

   d. Ø

7. _____ squid once before that, but it made me sick.

   a. I'd eaten

   b. I hadn't eaten

   c. I've ate

   d. I'd like to eat

8. The Rio Grande is the border between _____.

   a. the Mexico and the Texas

   b. the Mexico and Texas

   c. Mexico and the Texas

   d. Mexico and Texas

9. Before she _____ in Moscow, she _____ in Kiev.

   a. had lived . . . lived

   b. lived . . . lived

   c. lived . . . had lived

   d. lived . . . has lived

10. _____ is the closest planet to _____.

    a. The Venus . . . the earth   c. Venus . . . the earth

    b. Venus . . . an earth   d. A Venus . . . earth

11. _____ live music before you went to the concert?

    a. Did you ever heard   c. Had you ever heared

    b. Had you ever heard   d. Had ever you heard

12. The fiftieth state in _____.

    a. the United States is the Hawaii   c. United States is the Hawaii

    b. the United States is Hawaii   d. United States is Hawaii

13. That is _____ silliest thing you have ever said. It never snows in Miami.

    a. the   c. an

    b. a   d. some

14. _____ SUNY, is a large university system in New York.

    a. The State University of New York, or the   c. State University of the New York, or the

    b. The State University of New York, or   d. State University of New York, or

15. He _____ her before he saw her at the party.

    a. already had meet   c. had already met

    b. already has met   d. has already met

EDITING PRACTICE

Questions 16–30: Identify the *one* underlined word or phrase that must be changed for the sentence to be grammatically correct.

16. (a) The Philippines are a group of (b) islands located in (c) the South Pacific, north of (d) the Indonesia.

17. (a) After I (b) had made my daughter (c) a dress for her birthday, I baked a cake. She loved (d) a dress because it was silk.

18. I (a) have decided to go to (b) the University of California before I (c) received an acceptance letter from (d) Stanford.

19. (a) Grand Canyon is one of (b) the most popular of all (c) the national parks in (d) North America.

20. Before I (a) left home, my mother (b) had always cooked (c) a big meal for the whole family on (d) the Sundays.

21. One of (a) the Great Lakes that makes up part of the border between (b) Canada and (c) the United States is (d) the Lake Superior.

22. (a) Had you (b) eaten Italian food before you (c) had visited (d) Italy?

23. I (a) had eaten pizza (b) before I visited Italy, but I (c) no had (d) eaten Italian spinach pizza.

24. Usually I don't have (a) <u>an large appetite</u>, but we (b) <u>had walked</u> so far that I (c) <u>was starving</u> by (d) <u>the time</u> we got to the restaurant.

25. At (a) <u>the southern tip</u> of (b) <u>Vancouver Island</u> is (c) <u>the city</u> of (d) <u>the Victoria</u>.

26. I had (a) <u>the problems</u> with (b) <u>the homework</u>. (c) <u>Did you understand</u> the solution for (d) <u>number 5</u>?

27. (a) <u>The biology</u> includes (b) <u>the study</u> of (c) <u>plants</u> and (d) <u>animals</u>.

28. Before I (a) <u>had seen</u> the Alps, I (b) <u>had visited</u> (c) <u>the Andes Mountains</u> in (d) <u>South America</u>.

29. I (a) <u>had not read</u> (b) <u>an assignment</u> before class, so I (c) <u>didn't understand</u> what (d) <u>the professor</u> was talking about.

30. (a) <u>One of most interesting</u> school subjects is (b) <u>geography</u>. When I was young, I enjoyed studying about (c) <u>mountains</u>, (d) <u>rivers</u>, and different countries.

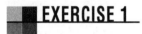

EXERCISE 1   *(Focus 1, page 314)*

Read the following sentences. If the focus of the sentence is on the subject, or *person* who performs the action, check (✓) the first box, or if the focus of the sentence is on the *result* of the action, check the second box.

FOCUS ON SUBJECT	FOCUS ON RESULT	
❏	❏	1. Unlike those in other countries, the U.S. government does not demand very much of its citizens.
❏	❏	2. A lot of Americans, however, are complaining nowadays that the government is intrusive.
❏	❏	3. But the U.S. government is not very restrictive.
❏	❏	4. People are allowed to express their opinions freely.
❏	❏	5. People are not required to carry personal identification with them.
❏	❏	6. Citizens are not required to vote.
❏	❏	7. Children are obligated to attend school until the age of 16. Is that intrusive?
❏	❏	8. Young people do not have to serve in the military—young men simply have to register.
❏	❏	9. Adult citizens must do one thing for their country: serve on a jury.

Complete the following letter, using the appropriate form of the passive voice in the simple past, past perfect, present perfect, or future.

Dear Julie,

The last time I wrote to you my life was very different. Do you remember that Charlie and I were thinking about leaving the city and moving far away? Well, we did it!

   Our decision to build our house in the North Woods of Canada (1) _____ (make) three years ago. The lumber (2) _____ (buy) and (3) _____ (move) by truck over miles of bad road. The plans for the house (4) _____ (draw up) on our dining room table. I was in charge of the work, but my contribution (5) _____ (limit) to giving orders. Most of the work was done by professionals, although a lot of the house (6) _____ (design) by Charlie. It's fabulous!

   The house (7) _____ (build) out of native Canadian pine in a large and beautiful field. The field (8) _____ (cover) with summer flowers when we arrived. I'm sorry to say that the flowers (9) _____ (cut) to make room for the house. Our puppy, Caesar, was very happy with his small dog house which Charlie built in the back yard. While we were all working on the house, we (10) _____ (visit) every day by some of the wild animals of northern Canada. We gave them names of Walt Disney characters. The deer (11) _____ (name) Bambi, the rabbit (12) _____ (call) Thumper, and a small gray wolf (13) _____ (nickname) Goofy. The skunk in our front yard (14) _____ (name) Flower. We built a fence to surround our two dozen acres of land. The house (15) _____ (finish) in four months, before the autumn frost, but the inside (16) _____ (*not* + paint) until the following spring.

Our furniture (17) _____ (send) from the city, and we (18) _____ (move) in by Halloween. But the only trick-or-treaters that (19) _____ (see) that year were two raccoons, a woodchuck, and a fox.

That was three years ago. . . . Since then we have decided to stay. Our apartment in the city (20) _____ (sell), our employers (21) _____ (notify) that we're not returning to work (even though Charlie and I (22) _____ (*just* + promote) when we decided to move), we told all our friends. Soon Charlie and I (23) _____ (*both* + employ) by different companies, but we (24) _____ (allow) to stay here at home and work at the computer.

I thought that it was going to be difficult for the children to adjust, but Jonathan, Lindsey, and Alex (25) _____ (*not* + bother) at all by the change. They have made new friends, and they love playing outside everyday. I love it because there's no traffic, polluted air, noise, or crime.

Well, Julie, I have to go. You're welcome to come up for a visit anytime.

Love,
Nancy

Read the following report from a local newspaper describing a car accident. As the editor, you have to decide which is more appropriate, active or passive voice, and put a check (✓) next to it. The first one has been done for you.

1. ___ A car accident injured a 7-year-old boy on Wednesday.

   ✓ A 7-year-old by was injured in a car accident on Wednesday.

2. ___ A bus was hit by the boy's father, Donald Derby, at the intersection of 1st Avenue and Spencer Street.

   ___ The boy's father, Donald Derby, hit a bus at the intersection of 1st Avenue and Spencer Street.

3. ___ A stop sign had been run by Derby.

   ___ Derby had run a stop sign.

4. ___ The boy was thrown through the car window.

   ___ The force of the accident threw the boy through the car window.

5. ___ Derby's daughter, Debbie, 3, was also in the car, but the broken glass did not cut her.

   ___ Derby's daughter, Debbie, 3, was also in the car, but she was not cut by the broken glass.

6. ___ An ambulance took the father to St. Christopher Hospital.

   ___ The father was taken to St. Christopher Hospital.

7. ___ The accident also injured the driver of the bus, Joe Barta.

   ___ The driver of the bus, Joe Barta, was also injured.

8. ___ An ambulance took him to Cedars Hospital, where doctors treated him.

   ___ He was taken to Cedars Hospital, where he was treated.

9. ___ Seat belts were not being worn by the Derbys at the time of the accident.

   ___ The Derbys were not wearing seat belts at the time of the accident.

10. ___ Derby will be charged with running a stop sign and driving without a license.

    ___ The police will charge Derby with running a stop sign and driving without a license.

Decide if the *by* + agent phrase is necessary in all of the following. Cross out the *by* phrases that you think are unnecessary.

It's that time of year again. Every night, gigantic sea turtles are coming out of the water and up onto the beach to lay their eggs. As soon as the turtles lay their eggs, the nests are covered with sand by the turtles, and then they go back into the sea. One of nature's mysteries, they return to the same place every year.

Early every morning before sunrise, marine biologists and volunteers go up and down the beach, looking for new nests. The nests are moved by them to a safer, darker area. The reason for this is that baby sea turtles are attracted by bright light. If there's a building with bright lights on the beach, the babies will go toward the building, instead of going toward the ocean, where they should be going. After the nests are moved by the people, the chances that the turtles will survive are increased by the people.

People can see a sea turtle by participating in a turtle watch between May and August. A turtle watch is held every night by The Department of Natural Resources. Reservations are required by them.

The sea turtle is protected by state and federal laws. People are being warned by officials to stay away from sea-turtle nests. If a person is caught by someone taking or bothering a sea turtle, its eggs, or its nest, that person will be fined $20,000 by the government, and he or she could spend a year in prison. There's a Sea Turtle Hot Line that people should call if a baby turtle is seen by them going away from the ocean.

(Based on "Sea turtles hit beaches in Broward," by Alan Topelson, *The Miami Herald*, May 1, 1993.)

Use the cues at the left to make sentences with the *get*-passive. The sentences are to help you decide which tense to use. The first one has been done for you.

Linda is a very busy working mother, but no matter how much work she does, she always gets her housework done, too.

1. clean/house The house gets cleaned. _____

2. cook/meals _____

3. do/dishes _____

At this time, many things are being done to improve our city. For example,

4. design/parks _____

5. renovate/historic buildings _____

6. build/housing for poor people _____

Every year our college does general repairs. These are some things that were done last year.

7. paint/classrooms _____

8. plant/trees _____

9. remodel/the cafeteria _____

Many companies are trying to decide how they are going to deal with global competition. Some companies have decided that several changes will be made for next year. What changes will be made?

10. cut/salaries _____

11. lay off/employees _____

12. not hire/new employees _____

Complete the following story with the *be*-passive or the *get*-passive and the past participle of the verb. The first one has been done for you.

A WEIRD WEDDING

Bea Prepared and Larry Lucky got married last week. Some unexpected events happened during Bea and Larry's wedding and honeymoon.

First, one week before the wedding, the minister _got transferred_ (transfer) to a new church, so they had to find a replacement at the last minute. After that, Larry _____ (lay off) unexpectedly. Then, on the night before the wedding, Bea _____ (poison) from the fish she _____ (serve) for dinner.

On the day of the wedding, the flowers _____ (not deliver) because the florist _____ (lose) on the way to the church. During the ceremony, the organist _____ (confuse) and played the funeral march instead of the wedding march. Also, the bride's dress _____ (tear) when the groom accidentally stepped on it. Then the ceremony _____ (interrupt) when a mouse came running through the church. The bridesmaids _____ (scare) and began to scream.

After the wedding ceremony, the reception _____ (hold) outdoors, but it started to rain and everyone got wet. Bea and Larry went to Las Vegas for their honeymoon, but their luggage _____ (put) on a flight to Hawaii.

PHRASAL VERBS

 EXERCISE 1 *(Focus 1, page 330)*

Using the pictures as cues, complete each sentence with a phrasal verb. Make sure the verbs agree in person and tense. The first one has been done for you.

1. Yesterday was Saturday, so Patrick _____got up_____ late.

2. He (not) _____ his clothes right away.

3. Instead, he _____ in his comfortable chair, read the newspaper, and drank some coffee.

4. Finally he _____ the coffee and got dressed.

5. Maurine is a kindergarten teacher. You might think she has an easy job, but every day after school she _____ her own classroom.

6. First, she _____ all of the toys.

7. Then she _____ her lesson plans for the next day.

8. When she finishes everything, she _____ the lights and goes home.

EXERCISE 2   (Focus 2, page 331)

Read the story. Then write each underlined phrasal verb next to its meaning below. Number 10 has been done for you as an example.

When I <u>woke up</u> this morning I was glad it was Saturday. Then I remembered that I had homework to do for Monday. Last week my teacher gave me an assignment to <u>find out</u> about burial customs around the world and <u>write up</u> a report about them. I <u>put off</u> doing my research for a whole week. Now I have to <u>hand in</u> my report on Monday. I <u>got out</u> my notebook and my pencil, but then I realized I didn't know anything about burial customs. I <u>put on</u> my clothes and decided that I should go to the public library and <u>look up</u> some information.

On the way to the library I <u>met up</u> with my friend Brittany. She wanted to <u>go out</u> shopping. When I explained what I had to do, she offered to <u>help me out</u>.

1. postpone _____

2. search for _____

3. write _____

4. dress _____

5. assist _____

6. research _____

7. give to a teacher _____

8. encountered _____

9. go _____

10. stopped sleeping <u>woke up</u>

11. took from its place _____

Complete each sentence by writing the phrasal verb and the object that best completes the sentence. The first one has been done for you.

1. Angela _____ turns _____ _____ on _____ the _____ radio _____.

2. She likes to listen to music while she _____ _____ her
   _____ and _____ _____ the trash.

3. But the music is too loud. Her mother says, "Angela _____ _____
   that _____!"

4. So Angela _____ _____ the radio and _____
   _____ the _____.

5. **Mr. Smith:** "Ms. Falco, I know we _____ _____ a meeting last week to discuss the contract, but I'm afraid we'll have to _____ _____ the _____ until next week—I have an unexpected emergency at the office."

6. **Ms. Falco:** "That's no problem. I'll contact the other members and _____ _____ the _____ for today. Should I _____ _____ another meeting for next week the same time?"

Mr. Smith: "That would be great."

■ EXERCISE 4   *(Focus 4, page 335)*

Rewrite the sentences in Exercise 3 with the object between the verb and the particle. The first one has been done for you.

1. <u>Angela turns the radio on.</u>

   or <u>Angela turns it on.</u>

2. _____

   _____

3. _____

   _____

4. _____

   _____

5. _____

   _____

6. _____

   _____

Replace each underlined object with a pronoun. Rewrite the sentences with the pronoun between the verb and the particle if possible.

Example: I just got over a <u>cold</u>, and then I got the flu.
I just got over a cold, and then I got the flu. (inseparable verb, not possible)

Don't throw out all of those <u>newspapers</u>; recycle them!
Don't throw them out; recycle them!

1. She was feeling sad, so we tried to cheer up <u>Janet</u>.
   _____

2. I called up <u>Janet</u> at work, and I could tell something was wrong.
   _____

3. She said she was having a bad day. This morning when she turned on <u>her new TV</u>, nothing happened.
   _____

4. She thought she would have to take <u>the TV</u> back to the store.
   _____

5. Maybe she could get by with <u>her old TV</u>.
   _____

6. This afternoon, I ran into a friend of mine who repairs <u>TVs</u>.
   _____

7. He went to Janet's house and went over <u>the TV</u> carefully.
   _____

8. Janet said, "I don't want to throw out <u>the TV</u>.
   _____

9. My friend found out <u>the problem</u>.
   _____

10. He came across a loose wire in <u>the electrical cord</u>.
    _____

For each of the following phrasal verbs, write two sentences using the noun phrases on the right as cues. Separate the verb when possible.

Example: pick up   it
                        a package at the post office

Anne had to pick it up.
Anne had to pick up a package at the post office.

turn off   them
                all the electrical appliances before going on vacation.

1. _____

2. _____

call up   my family
               them

3. _____

4. _____

get off   the horse
               it

5. _____

6. _____

take off   my wet shoes and socks
               them

7. _____

8. _____

look up   it
               the new address of the movie theater

9. _____

10. _____

run into   her parents
               them

11. _____

12. _____

Take turns with a partner asking and answering the following questions.

1. Where did you grow up?

2. Did you ever show up late for dinner? What did your mother say?

3. Did you ever come home late? Did your parents punish you?

4. How often does your family eat out?

5. What is something that you wanted but got by without when you were a child?

6. What American customs will never catch on in your country?

7. How did you get to school today?

8. Can you fix a car that has broken down?

9. Have you ever passed out?

ADJECTIVE CLAUSES AND PARTICIPLES AS ADJECTIVES

EXERCISE 1   *(Focus 1, page 350)*

The following words are used to describe people. Unscramble the words given below to finish the description of these people.

Example: an / in / is / is / extremist / some / someone / way / who
      A fanatic *is someone who is an extremist in some way.*

1. a /about / is / likes / other / people / talk / that / to / person
   A gossip _____
   _____

2. ages / and / are / are / between / nineteen / of / people / the / thirteen / who / young
   Teenagers _____
   _____

3. are / from / money / or / pocket / purse / steal / who / thieves / your
   Pickpockets_____
   _____

4. are / better / else / everyone / people / than / that / they're / think
   Snobs_____
   _____

5. alcohol / doesn't / someone / drink / is / who
   A teetotaler _____
   _____

6. everything / is / knows / (s)he / someone / that / thinks
   A know-it-all _____
   _____

7. a / army / has / in / is / lowest / rank / soldier / that / the / the
   A private _____
   _____

8. a / an / individual / is / lot / of / spends / time / TV / watching / who

   A couch potato _____

   _____

9. are / are / elderly / people / who

   Senior citizens _____

   _____

10. is / a / person / that / is / famous

    A celebrity _____

    _____

 EXERCISE 2   *(Focus 2, page 352)*

Using one word/group of words from each column, write a complete sentence. Numbers 1–6 are conversational definitions of animals, meaning they're *informal*. Numbers 7–12 on the next page are textbook definitions, meaning they're *formal*. The first one has been done for you. Be sure to use all the words/phrases at least one time.

CONVERSATIONAL DEFINITIONS:

Cockroaches	a big wild animal	people are afraid of
Dogs	a colorful bird	people don't like to see in their home
Piranhas	a wild animal	we call "man's best friend"
The monkey	bugs	we see in hot climates
The parrot	fish	we see living in ice and snow
The polar bear	pets	we see in the jungle, swinging through the trees

1. <u>Cockroaches are bugs that people don't like to see in their home.</u>

   _____

2. _____

   _____

3. _____

   _____

4. _____

   _____

5. _____

   _____

6. _____

   _____

WRITTEN DEFINITIONS:

Cockroaches	a mammal	exterminators are constantly trying to eradicate
Dogs	a multi-colored bird	scientists classify as the canine species
Piranhas	a primate	scientists have determined to be related to human beings
The monkey	domestic animals	we call carnivores, or meat-eating animals
The parrot	fish	we find inhabiting the arctic regions
The polar bear	insects	we find inhabiting tropical jungles

7. _____

8. _____

9. _____

10. _____

11. _____

12. _____

What differences—besides the use of *that* and *which*—do you see between the formal and informal definitions?

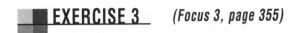

EXERCISE 3   *(Focus 3, page 355)*

Circle the correct adjective, choosing between the underlined words.

Sandy and Victor, both English teachers, lived abroad for many years, first in Saudi Arabia, and then in the Far East, where, like many (1) <u>experienced / experiencing</u> travelers, they suffered from culture shock. Recently they returned to the United States and experienced something that is called reverse culture shock. They had lived abroad for a very long time, and everything back home was new for them.

The cars seemed so big, and the people did too. They had forgotten how many overweight Americans there were. But everyone was (2) <u>obsessed/obsessing</u> with dieting; they thought about it all the time. Every magazine seemed to have an article about dieting, but not many people seemed (3) <u>disciplined/disciplining</u> enough to follow a diet. Most were (4) <u>disappointed/disappointing</u> dieters.

When Sandy and Victor had first arrived in Saudi Arabia, it was (5) <u>surprised/surprising</u> to see the Arab women (6) <u>covered/covering</u> from head to toe. Sandy was equally (7) <u>shocked/shocking</u> when she returned to the United States and saw women wearing rollers in public.

And both Sandy and Victor were (8) <u>frustrated/frustrating</u> because they didn't have a car. When they lived abroad, transportation had never been a problem, but the North American city that they lived in had very poor public transportation; sometimes they had to wait an hour for the bus. It was very (9) <u>annoyed/annoying</u>. And the bus stop was almost a mile from their apartment, so they had to walk a lot, too. At the end of the day, they were (10) <u>exhausted/exhausting</u>.

It's difficult to return home after being in another country for a while. At first, Sandy and Victor were (11) <u>worried/worrying</u> that they had a negative attitude about everything, but they felt (12) <u>relieved/relieving</u> to hear about reverse culture shock. It will take time to feel comfortable living here again.

■EXERCISE 4 (Focus 3, page 355)

Have you experienced culture shock? How about reverse culture shock? Write about your own experiences by completing the following sentences. Use the -ed or -ing form of the word in parentheses. If any of these adjectives don't reflect your own feelings or experiences, feel free to replace them with -ed or -ing forms that do.

1. I was (surprise) when I first saw _____

2. It was (frustrate) to _____

3. I was (confuse) when _____

4. It was (excite) to _____

5. I was (worry) that _____

6. It was (frighten) when _____

7. It was (fascinate) to see _____

8. I was (embarrass) when _____

9. I was (annoy) when _____

10. I felt (relieve) when _____

CONDITIONALS

EXERCISE 1   *(Focus 1, page 364)*

The following passage is about Constantine, a Romanian immigrant who lives in California and drives a taxi. Fill in the blanks with *hypothetical conditionals*. Be careful—some are negative.

1. Constantine doesn't really want to live here, but because of political problems, he can't live in Romania. If politics _____ (be) different, Constantine _____ (have) to live in another country.

2. Constantine has to live abroad—he can't live in Romania. He _____ (live) in his apartment in Bucharest if he _____ (have) to live abroad.

3. Constantine has a hard life in California; life is much easier in Romania. He _____ (have) a comfortable life if he _____ (live) in Bucharest.

4. He doesn't know much English, so he works as a taxi driver. If he _____ (know) more English, Constantine _____ (work) as an engineer; he _____ (work) as a taxi driver.

5. Constantine learned his English on the street. His English is OK, but if he _____ (go) to school, he _____ (learn) more English, especially how to read and write.

6. Constantine shares a small apartment with four other Romanians—he can't afford a nice place. He _____ (live) in a nice apartment if he _____ (have) a decent job.

7. Constantine's life is even more difficult because he's waiting for political asylum. His life _____ (be) easier if he _____ (have) to wait for political asylum—it's been three years.

8. Constantine is not a legal resident of the country, so he can't bring his family here. If he _____ (be) a resident, he _____ (bring) his family to the United States.

9. He's not very happy because his family lives so far away. He _____ (be) happier if he _____ (bring) his family to live here.

10. Constantine's wife is in Bucharest, taking care of the family alone. If she _____ (be) here, she _____ (have) Constantine's help.

Rewrite the hypothetical conditionals from Exercise 1, changing the order of the clauses. Be careful with punctuation.

1. _____
   _____
2. _____
   _____
3. _____
   _____
4. _____
   _____
5. _____
   _____
6. _____
   _____
7. _____
   _____
8. _____
   _____
9. _____
   _____
10. _____
    _____

EXERCISE 3   *(Focus 2, page 366)*

Complete the following hypothetical conditional sentences. Then rewrite the sentences, changing the order of the clauses.

1. I'd be a millionaire if _____
2. If I had more free time, _____
3. If I were you, _____
4. She would buy that if _____
5. If my house were on fire, _____
6. I'd travel around the world if _____
7. If I could change one thing about my life, _____

8. I wouldn't do that if _____

9. If I could make three wishes, _____

10. I would be a better student if _____

EXERCISE 4   *(Focus 3, page 367)*

The following people are thinking about their past and how different individuals and events changed their lives. The pairs of sentences express what really happened in the past. Write hypothetical conditionals based on these sentences. The first sentence in the pair should be used in the *if* clause.

Example: Mary went to the Bahamas on her vacation. That's where she met Gordon.
If Mary hadn't gone to the Bahamas, she wouldn't have met Gordon.

1. Mary met Gordon. That's why she didn't marry her high-school sweetheart.

   _____

   _____

2. Gordon went to medical school. Because of that, he didn't go to law school.

   _____

   _____

3. Gordon became a doctor. As a result, he didn't become a lawyer.

   _____

   _____

4. Claudia had Mr. Stack for algebra. Because of him, she passed math and she graduated from high school.

   _____

   _____

5. Mr. Stack was Claudia's teacher. As a result, she didn't quit school.

   _____

   _____

6. Barb married Tom. Because of him, she moved to Toronto.

   _____

   _____

7. Barb knew how to speak French and Spanish. That's why she got a job with an airline.

   _____

   _____

8. Jan got pneumonia. That's why she moved to Arizona.

   _____

   _____

9. Jan moved to Arizona. That's where she learned to ride a horse.

   _____

   _____

10. There wasn't birth control years ago. My grandmother had 12 children.

    _____

    _____

How did different people and events change *your* life? Write three hypothetical conditionals about your own past.

11. _____

    _____

12. _____

    _____

13. _____

    _____

■ EXERCISE 5   *(Focus 3, page 367)*

Write hypothetical conditionals based on the following sentences.

Example: I didn't know that you needed me, so I went home.
          If I had known that you needed me, I wouldn't have gone home.

1. I didn't give her the message because I didn't see her.

   _____

   _____

2. I wasn't able to go with you last weekend because I didn't have any money.

   _____

   _____

3. I didn't know you were in the hospital, so I didn't visit you.

   _____

   _____

4. We got into trouble because we broke the law.

   _____

   _____

5. I didn't know we were going to be so late, so I didn't call you.

   _____

   _____

6. I ate the cookies because they were there.

_____

_____

7. You made a lot of mistakes because you weren't careful.

_____

_____

8. Lexi wasn't at the meeting, so we weren't able to solve the problem.

_____

_____

9. I didn't have a car, so I took the subway.

_____

_____

10. You told me the news, so I knew.

_____

_____

EXERCISE 6   (Focus 4, page 371)

Three men have proposed to Eva. She doesn't know if she should marry Mack, Sato, or Travis. The following are predictions about her life. Make future conditional sentences using *if* and the verbs below.

Example: marry Sato ➜ move to Tokyo
If she marries Sato, she'll move to Tokyo.

SATO = JAPAN

1. move to Tokyo ➜ have to learn Japanese _____

_____

2. learn Japanese ➜ be the first one in her family to learn another language _____

_____

MACK = HOMETOWN

3. marry Mack ➜ stay in Fremont, her hometown _____

_____

4. live in Fremont ➜ not have to learn another language _____

_____

5. not leave Fremont ➜ her life not change very much _____

_____

TRAVIS = MONEY

6. marry Travis ➜ be rich _____

_____

7. live in a mansion ➜ feel like a princess _____

_____

8. not feel like herself ➜ lose control over her life _____

_____

9. marry Sato or Travis ➜her life be more exciting _____

_____

10. not get married ➜ not have to worry about this _____

_____

EXERCISE 7   *(Focus 5, page 373)*

Complete the following sentences and check (✓) the correct box to indicate if the sentence is a future conditional or a hypothetical conditional. Don't forget to add a comma where necessary.

future   hypothetical

❏   ❏   1. If the rain stops soon _____

_____

❏   ❏   2. What would you do if _____

_____

❏   ❏   3. If you ever do that again _____

_____

❏   ❏   4. If I were in her shoes _____

_____

❏   ❏   5. I wouldn't do that if _____

_____

❏   ❏   6. He wouldn't say that if _____

_____

❏   ❏   7. If you gave me a million dollars _____

_____

❏   ❏   8. I will leave the tip if _____

_____

❏   ❏   9. If I never see you again _____

_____

future	hypothetical	
❏	❏	10. If you go barefoot _____
		_____
❏	❏	11. I will say "You're welcome" if _____
		_____
❏	❏	12. If you really loved me _____
		_____
❏	❏	13. My teacher will become angry if _____
		_____
❏	❏	14. If people stop fighting wars _____
		_____
❏	❏	15. I would be very happy if _____
		_____
❏	❏	16. Oh, darling. If you leave me _____
		_____

EXERCISE 8   (Focus 5, page 373)

Put a check (✓) next to the sentences that are hypothetical (i.e., the situation probably won't happen).

1. ____ I would move to Montana if I won the lottery.

2. ____ If I don't find a job here, I'm going to move to Seattle.

3. ____ If Peggy were tall, she wouldn't have to look up at people.

4. ____ Tom's going to marry Barb if he gets a promotion.

5. ____ Tom would marry Barb if he made more money.

6. ____ We wouldn't have these problems if we spoke Japanese.

7. ____ If you go to Japan, you'll be able to practice your Japanese.

8. ____ I won't go with you if you wear that outfit.

9. ____ If they don't pay him more, he'll quit his job.

10. ____ Jo would quit her job if the company transferred her.

Use the words in the list to complete the following factual-conditional sentences.

ask for a doggy bag	make a reservation
ask for the check	order an appetizer
ask for the manager	order another round
don't eat your food in the restaurant	the service is all right
like it cooked very little	want more coffee

1. If you're planning to go to a popular restaurant, you should _____
   _____

2. You order take-out if you _____
   _____

3. When you buy everyone at your table a drink, you _____
   _____

4. You ask for a refill if you _____
   _____

5. If you want to eat something before the main course (or entrée), you _____
   _____

6. You order your meat rare if you _____
   _____

7. When you are ready to pay, you _____
   _____

8. If you want to take the rest of your meal home, you _____
   _____

9. You leave the server a 15 percent tip if _____
   _____

10. When you have a complaint, you _____
    _____

CROSSWORD PUZZLE

If you need help completing this crossword puzzle, ask a native speaker of English.

SUPERSTITIONS

ACROSS

1. _____ never strikes twice in the same place

9. U.S. government organization that regulates airlines (abbrev.)

10. One (Spanish)

12. If you hurt yourself, you say, "_____!"

14. The front of your leg between the ankle and the knee (plural)

15. If your job is to create good impressions of an organization with the public, then you work in _____ (abbr.)

16. If a kitten is hungry, it will _____.

18. If you go to Hawaii, you will be welcomed with a _____ around your neck.

19. If your name was Adam, then you lived with Eve in the Garden of _____.

21. My sister was hurt at work, so she _____ the company, because they didn't have any safety regulations.

22. If you pass under a ladder, you will have _____ luck.

23. If you want someone to go away, tell him to take a _____.

25. All right

27. Same as 6 Down

30. I made a wish on a falling star, but it hasn't come true _____.

31. North Carolina (abbr.)

32. If you _____ salt, throw some of it over your shoulder to avoid bad luck.

33. Blood type

34. If the score is 2-2, we call it a _____.

36. If you nail a _____ over your door, it will bring you good luck.

DOWN

2. You will have bad luck _____ you open an umbrella indoors.

3. If it's not a liquid or a solid, it's a _____.

4. If you think something is funny, you say _____.

5. Religious sisters

6. If you are familiar with all the details of a situation, then you know all of the _____ and outs.

7. If you don't want any, just say "_____, thank you."

8. For good luck on her wedding day, a bride needs _____ old, _____ new, _____ borrowed, and _____ blue.

11. _____ 13th is an unlucky day. (2 words)

13. Marry

15. Urinate (slang)

17. If you are gone for fourteen days, then I'll be two _____ without you.

18. Whenever Masaya gambles in Las Vegas, he wins. He's a very _____ guy.

20. You will have bad luck if a black _____ passes in front of you.

24. If a company is incorporated, it will have this abbreviation at the end of its name.

26. Prefix meaning *air, gas,* or *aviation.*

28. Gorillas and monkeys

29. If you like dark beer, then you might not like _____. (plural)

32. If you want to show respect to a man, you can call him "_____."

34 & 35. Opposite of *from*

EXERCISE 11   (Focus 6, page 375)

Match the following to make complete sentences.

1. If you make something up, _____
2. When you make believe, _____
3. If you make dinner, _____
4. You talk when you _____
5. If you make off with something, you _____
6. Something is logical when it _____
7. If you make something over, _____
8. When you're successful, you _____

a. it's renovated, or like new.
b. made it.
c. make a speech.
d. makes sense.
e. steal.
f. you're lying.
g. you cook.
h. you pretend.

EXERCISE 12   (Focus 7, page 376)

Use the words in the list to complete the following sentences.

he might have died	I had the flu
I call the doctor today	I see anything out of the ordinary
I felt a lump in my breast	the doctors hadn't cured her cancer
I hadn't quit smoking years ago	you have the chills
I might have gotten seriously ill	

1. I would call my doctor immediately if _____

2. If my father hadn't called 911 as soon as he did, _____

3. I will call my doctor and make an appointment if _____

4. I may not get an appointment for a couple of weeks if _____

5. I might have gotten bronchitis or lung cancer if _____

6. If I hadn't been vaccinated, _____

7. I might stay in bed and call in sick if _____

8. You may have a fever if _____

9. My mother wouldn't be alive today if _____

TEST PREP

Choose the word or phrase (*a, b, c,* or *d*) that best completes each sentence. Then circle the letter.

1. Tortillas, the bread of Mexico, _____ with ground corn, water, and lime.

   a. are being made   c. get made

   b. are made   d. make

2. Many Mexicans buy their tortillas and take them home. They _____ at their local *tortillería*, where they are produced by machine.

   a. eat out them   c. pick up them

   b. eat them out   d. pick them up

3. Other Mexicans, _____ could buy them, prefer to make their own fresh, hot tortillas at home.

   a. that   c. who

   b. which   d. whose

4. Many women _____ the dough, or *masa*, between their hands and flatten it into a thin, round pancake-like shape.

   a. are taken   c. have been taken

   b. are taking   d. take

5. The tortilla _____ in Mexico for centuries, since the days of the Aztecs.

   a. are eaten   c. has been eaten

   b. has been eating   d. is eaten

6. Marcia gets _____ very early, before sunrise, so when she gets dressed, it's still dark.

   a. off   c. out

   b. on   d. up

7–8. This morning she must've been very _____ when she _____ her clothes.

   a. tire   a. got dressed

   b. tired   b. got on

   c. tires   c. put on

   d. tiring   d. took off

9. As usual, her friend _____ and they rode to work together.

   a. picked her up   c. ran into her

   b. picked up her   d. ran her over

10. Marcia was giving a presentation at work when she noticed that everyone looked very _____.

   a. amuse
   b. amused
   c. amuses
   d. amusing

11. Later on she _____ why everyone had been smiling during her presentation.

   a. showed up
   b. found out
   c. went over
   d. passed out

12. She had just finished talking on the phone, and as she _____, Marcia looked down at her feet.

   a. held on
   b. hung on
   c. hung up
   d. put off

13. She realized that she was wearing a blue shoe on her left foot and a brown shoe on her right foot; she had _____ the wrong shoes.

   a. caught on
   b. thrown out
   c. taken off
   d. put on

14. Even if she lives to be one hundred years old, Marcia _____ forget that day.

   a. isn't going
   b. wouldn't
   c. will never
   d. might

15. Poor Marcia! All of us have had _____ moments, but they are not all as memorable as hers.

   a. embarrassable
   b. embarrassed
   c. embarrassful
   d. embarrassing

EDITING PRACTICE

Questions 16–25: Find the *one* underlined word or phrase (*a, b, c,* or *d*) that needs to be changed to make the sentence correct.

16. Two tourists (a) <u>were</u> (b) <u>being</u> robbed while they (c) <u>were</u> checking (d) <u>into</u> the Sandy Shores Hotel last Saturday night.

17. The couple (a) <u>had</u> (b) <u>been</u> left their luggage unattended, and when they (c) looked <u>up</u>, the bags (d) <u>had</u> disappeared.

18. When the police showed (a) <u>off</u>, they said that the bags (b) <u>could have been</u> stolen (c) <u>by</u> the same criminals (d) <u>who</u> have been robbing foreign tourists in the area.

19. The police also pointed (a) <u>out</u> that the thief might be someone (b) <u>which</u> works at one of the hotels, or it (c) <u>could be</u> someone (d) <u>who's dressed</u> like a tourist.

20. Every year tourists around the world (a) <u>are</u> (b) <u>robbed</u> like this, because they become careless. If they (c) <u>will take</u> their eyes (d) <u>off</u> their luggage, something like this might occur.

21. South Dakota is (a) <u>knowing</u> (b) <u>for</u> Mount Rushmore, where the enormous heads of four U.S. presidents (c) <u>are</u> (d) <u>carved</u> in the side of a mountain.

22. Korczak Ziolkowski, (a) <u>who</u> (b) <u>was</u> (c) <u>died</u> in 1982, helped carve Mt. Rushmore, and then bought a nearby mountain where he (d) <u>began to</u> carve a gigantic replica of the Sioux Chief Crazy Horse.

23. Ziolkowski's widow, Ruth, said that the sculpture was her husband's dream and that a strange relationship (a) <u>had existed</u> between him and Crazy Horse: he (b) <u>was</u> (c) <u>born</u> on the same day that Crazy Horse (d) <u>passed out</u>, but 31 years later.

24. She (a) <u>will never</u> get (b) <u>over</u> her husband's death, but it is (c) <u>inspired</u> to think that his spirit and Crazy Horse's are in heaven. If they (d) <u>are</u>, they're probably watching the construction together.

25. The Ziolkowski family has continued to work on the huge project, and if they don't run (a) <u>over</u> any problems, it (b) <u>could</u> be many years before the sculpture is (c) <u>finished</u>—their great grandchildren (d) <u>might</u> see a completed Crazy Horse.